KU-204-567

CONTENTS

WHAT'S IN YOUR GUIDEBOOK?

Independent authors Impartial, up-to-date information from our travel experts who meticulously source local knowledge.

Experience Thomas Cook's 165 years in the travel industry and guidebook publishing enriches every word with expertise you can trust.

Travel know-how Contributions by thousands of staff around the globe, each one living and breathing travel.

Editors Travel-publishing professionals, pulling everything together to craft a perfect blend of words, pictures, maps and design.

You, the traveller We deliver a practical, no-nonsense approach to information, geared to how you really use it.

ABOUT THE AUTHOR

Debbie Stowe is the author of more than a dozen travel and non-fiction books. A freelance journalist, she writes on topics from travel and the natural world to social and cultural issues. She lives in Bucharest.

● *Experience the tranquillity of the Maldives*

Indian Ocean

O Muli
MEEMU ATOLL

LAAMU ATOLL
Hadhdhunmathi Atoll
O Hithadhoo

South Nilandhe Atoll
DHAALU ATOLL
Kudahuvadhoo O

THAA ATOLL
Kolhumadulu Atoll
Veymandhoo O

GAAF ALIF ATOLL
North Huvadhu Atoll

O Viligili

*Huvadhoo Kandu
(One and a Half Degree Channel)*

Thinadhoo O
GAAF DHAAL ATOLL
South Huvadhu Atoll

Addu Kandu (Equatorial Channel)

GNAVIYANI ATOLL O Fuamulaku
Fuvahmulah Atoll

Hithadhoo O O *Addu Atoll*
SEENU ATOLL O Gan

Equator

N

India

Maldives

Getting to know the Maldives

As dream holiday destinations go, the Maldives must rank pretty high on the list. Year-round sun, Robinson Crusoe-style desert islands and an azure sea that is home to a vibrant underwater world are more usually the stuff of holiday brochures than real life. Not here, though. Honeymooners, couples on their trip of a lifetime and scuba divers are all drawn to the tropical paradise of this extraordinary archipelago.

Almost 1,200 small islands make up the Maldives. Two hundred are home to local people, with around another 100 that are either already catering to tourists or will be in the near future. Many are so small that they can be crossed on foot in minutes. Only by flying above does the visitor really grasp the amazing geography of this Indian Ocean country; the deep vast blue of the sea is speckled with occasional golden patches of sand, often dense with palm trees.

The country is one of contrasts. A strict Islamic state, every Maldivian is a Muslim by law. Local people are banned from drinking alcohol, and many women cover their heads with a *buruga*. Meanwhile, a little way across the sea, bikini-clad tourists knock back cocktails at the beach bar, served by barmen who have never tasted the drinks they mix. It's certainly not as easy to sample the local culture here as it is in other tourist destinations on the Indian subcontinent. You could spend your whole two weeks without coming into contact with a Maldivian coin or banknote, and not see any sign of the religion that dominates here. But the cultural side is there if you want to seek it out.

However, for most tourists what the Maldives provides is simply a fantastic beach holiday, offering many of the best points of the Indian subcontinent without the hassles. Beaches and water are both pristine. Whichever resort you end up at, both service and food are likely to be exemplary. With only a limited number of guests on each island, you will never find yourself jostling for towel space on a crowded patch of sand. Divers have one of the most varied and stunning marine environments right on their doorstep (and the water is always warm). And though perfection like this doesn't come cheap, it offers excellent value. Which is why some holidaymakers come back for their trip of a lifetime year after year.

△ *Paradise Island lives up to its name*

THE BEST OF THE MALDIVES

A tropical paradise worthy of the name, the Maldives' chief draw is its astonishing beauty. Gentle waves lapping at white sands provide the ideal backdrop for annual R&R, while the sea offers scuba divers a range of vivid and fascinating marine life. Whatever you're seeking from the Maldives, you'll enjoy it in postcard-perfect serenity.

TOP 10 ATTRACTIONS

- **Ithaa Undersea Restaurant on Conrad Maldives Rangali Island (Ari Atoll)** Dine amid the fishes at the world's first underwater restaurant (see page 59).

- **Diving at Fotteyo Kandu (Vaavu Atoll)** Caves, corals and a cornucopia of marine life at one of the Maldives' best dive sites (see page 71).

- **Foodies and fresh fish fans** will enjoy the eye-catching produce on view at Malé's bustling fish market (see page 43).

- **Café life in Malé** A stroll around the capital's cafés will give you an authentic glimpse of this relaxed nation at leisure (see page 46).

- **Seaplane flight** Nowhere does the Maldives look more spectacular than from a Twin Otter seaplane 760 m (2,500 ft) above the sea (see page 25).

- **Village life in Villingili (North Malé)** Somersaulting children and local men shinning trees in pursuit of coconuts present an absorbing contrast to resort life (see page 31).

- **Dinner on the beach** Waves gently lapping at the shore, the moon up above and gastronomic delights brought to your table – what could be more perfect (see pages 35 and 68)?

- **Republic Day celebrations** Enjoy the pomp and colour as the locals celebrate their country's republican status (see page 103).

- **Perfect beaches** abound in the Maldives – but those on the 'picnic islands' of Ari Atoll are particularly stunning (see pages 51–2).

- **Spa at Soneva Fushi (Baa Atoll)** Pamper yourself with a self-indulgent spa at Soneva Fushi or one of the other havens of relaxation dotted around the atolls (see page 20).

○ *Laze by the ocean on North Malé Atoll*

SYMBOLS KEY

The following symbols are used throughout this book:

ⓐ address ⓣ telephone ⓦ website address ⓔ email
ⓛ opening times ⓘ important

The following symbols are used on the maps:

✉ post office   ◯ city
✈ airport   ◯ large town
✚ hospital   ○ small town
⛨ police station   ◼ POI (point of interest)
❶ numbers denote featured cafés, restaurants & evening venues

RESTAURANT CATEGORIES

The symbol after the name of each restaurant listed in this guide
indicates the price of a typical three-course meal without drinks.
£ = up to US$20   ££ = US$20–60   £££ = over US$60

▶ *Tourist boats whisk travellers to their dream resort*

RESORTS
Places under the sun

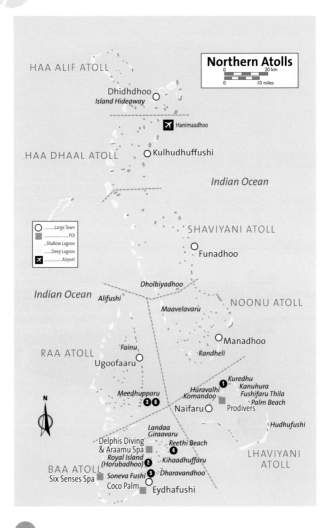

Northern Atolls

| 0 | 20 km |
| 0 | 10 miles |

HAA ALIF ATOLL

Dhidhdhoo
Island Hideaway

✈ Hanimaadhoo

HAA DHAAL ATOLL ○ Kulhudhuffushi

Indian Ocean

○ ....Large Town
■ ....POI
....Shallow Lagoon
....Deep Lagoon
✈ ....Airport

SHAVIYANI ATOLL

○ Funadhoo

Dholbiyadhoo

Indian Ocean *Alifushi*

Maavelavaru NOONU ATOLL

○ Manadhoo

RAA ATOLL *Fainu* *Randheli*

Ugoofaaru ○

Kuredhu
Kanuhura
Meedhupparu Huravalhi *Fushifaru Thila*
③ ⑥ Komandoo *Palm Beach*
Naifaru ○ Prodivers

Hudhufushi

Landaa
Giraavaru
Delphis Diving ■ *Reethi Beach*
& Araamu Spa ④
Royal Island ② *Kihaadhuffaru* LHAVIYANI
(Horubadhoo) ⑤ *Dharavandhoo* ATOLL
BAA ATOLL ■ *Soneva Fushi*
Six Senses Spa ■ Coco Palm
○ Eydhafushi

N

Northern Atolls

The Northern Atolls are one of the Maldives' main growth areas for tourism, with the current ten or so resorts set to almost double in the near future. Planned developments include the first incursions into virgin atolls, and are therefore likely to offer visitors even more in the way of peace and seclusion. Seeing, as it does, far less boat traffic than the busier atolls closer to the capital, the uppermost resorts enjoy even more pristine waters and pure air than can be found elsewhere in the archipelago.

New operations setting up here have to contend with nearly a hundred competitors throughout the country, so it's natural that they try to distinguish themselves by providing even more luxurious conditions and spectacular facilities. One such development is taking place at Island Hideaway, one of the country's newest resorts, which boasts the Maldives' first marina. This is designed to drum up more yacht trade. Yacht-based holidaymakers, such as Russian billionaire Roman Abramovich, are already regulars in the Northern Atolls, perhaps trying to escape the relatively busier areas nearer the capital. Those staying in the top-end resorts can expect to enjoy pampering of the highest order – from massages to butlers!

While it is possible that guests staying in the northern reaches (those without their own yachts, that is!) may be brought to their hotels with a speed-boat ride of over two hours, it is far more likely that the journey will be made by seaplane, taking somewhere in the region of half an hour.

BEACHES

With white sand, golden sun, azure waters and picturesque palms, this part of the country has the usual quota of fantastic beaches that you will find typical of the atolls of the Maldives. Their remoteness ensures that, if anything, they are even more pristine than their more central equivalents.

THINGS TO SEE & DO

Diving

The relatively recent arrival of tourism in the 1990s and smaller number of boats making their way around the atolls have kept the sites here unspoiled, and there is excellent diving to be done. The region yields plenty of diving – both kandu (channel) and thila (long oval reefs that are prone to currents). Thila dives in Raa and Baa Atolls, to the west of the southern groups of islands, include the protected marine area of Horubadhoo Thila, which is teeming with pelagic and schooling fish, plus the occasional grey reef shark and eagle ray. Other thilas in the area are Dharavandhoo, one of the most vivid, plus Beriyan Faru, Kottefaru Kuda and Vaadhoo, all of which are fairly challenging sites. From May to July the southwest monsoon brings out mantas and whale sharks. Strong currents in places mean that as a diving destination the Northern Atolls tend to suit the more experienced, although there are a few sites appropriate for novices too.

East of Baa and Raa, in Lhaviyani Atoll, you'll find in close proximity the remains of the *Skipjack II* and *Gaafaru*, fishing vessels that in their two decades of submersion have attracted significant marine life. The site is easily visible: the bow of *Skipjack II* protrudes clearly from the surface of the sea. There are two good giri dives (giri is a small patch of coral a couple of metres below the surface): Narcola, south of Huravalhi, which is rich in overhangs and crevices, and Maa, south-west of Kanuhuraa, where the many currents ensure fantastic marine diversity. The Kuredhu Express, another protected marine area, is an exhilarating drift dive, while the 200 m long (656 ft) Fushifaru Thila, with its strong currents, is an outstanding site for advanced divers.

Further north, where resorts are as yet thin on the ground, little is known of the potential dive sites, although as hotels start to open up, doubtless more will be discovered.

Delphis Diving Delphis can accommodate all divers from novices to experts. Beginners' classes are limited to five participants or fewer, and

⬥ *Work seems a world away*

the instructors try to keep all groups as small as possible. PADI and SSI courses are available. Dive sorties are made twice a day, following an initial orientation dive to assess your abilities, and a 15-minute introductory lesson is offered for free. One of the archipelago's few decompression chambers has recently been installed on Royal Island.

ⓐ Royal Island, Baa Atoll ❶ 660 0088 ⓦ www.delphisdiving.com
ⓔ ddcroy@delphis.com.mv ❷ 08.30–12.30, 14.00–18.00

Prodivers Two of the company's three dive sites are based on northern islands, at Kuredhu and Komandoo. The usual range of PADI courses are run, from beginner's courses right up to Divemaster. Taking its lead from adventure sports operators further west, the firm also promotes its own clothing line. Nitrox and night diving are possible here, and staff can also help out with photography equipment.

ⓐ Champa Building, Kandidhonmaniku Goalhi, Malé (head office)
❶ 662 0343 ⓦ www.prodivers.com ⓔ info@prodivers.com

Spas
Araamu Spa The orchid-rich spa on Royal Island is similar to the one on its sister resort, Sun Island, but on a smaller scale. Ayurveda inspires many of the treatments, and there is also a wellness centre. The pond nearby is said to have been used by the royal family who previously inhabited the isle and gave it its name.

ⓐ Royal Island, Baa Atoll ❶ 660 0088 ⓦ www.araamuspa.com
ⓔ royal@araamuspa.com ❷ 08.00–20.00

Coco Palm Using a variety of massage techniques including shiatsu, Thai, Balinese, Chinese, reflexology and aromatherapy, the spa provides a range of treatments and products for sale. Coco Palm Bodu Hithi, in North Malé Atoll, has an associated outlet.

ⓐ Coco Palm Dhuni Kolhu, Baa Atoll ❶ 660 0011 ⓦ www.cocopalm.com
ⓔ dhunikolhu@cocopalm.com.mv

⬥ *Lie back for some pampering*

Six Senses Spa One of the big-name spa operators active in the Maldives, Six Senses has branches in Asia, Europe, the Middle East and the Caribbean. The company takes a philosophical and holistic approach to spa treatment, using 'six spheres' of human experience. Whatever your thoughts about that, the Soneva Fushi outlet is hugely successful and has claimed various awards. It draws upon Western techniques, as well as Ayurvedic principles. Treatments, which cover both health and beauty, can also be taken in your own villa.

🅐 Soneva Fushi, Baa Atoll 🅣 660 0304 🅦 www.sixsenses.com
🅔 mgr-fushi@sixsensesspas.com

TAKING A BREAK

Cafés
Maldivian Tea House ££ ❶ Kuredhu has tried faithfully to bring the local café experience to its shores in the form of the straightforwardly named Maldivian Tea House, which serves up traditional short eats and curries. In an authentic touch no alcohol is served (although you can always make up for it in one of the island's six bars). 🅐 Kuredhu, Lhaviyani Atoll 🅣 662 0337 🅦 www.kuredu.com 🅔 reservations@kuredhu.com

Palm Terrace ££ ❷ Located next to the pool, Palm Terrace has an array of cocktails, mocktails and snacks, which can be enjoyed on poolside deckchairs. A civilised highlight is afternoon tea: your choice of Earl Grey, Darjeeling, peppermint and chamomile among others, served with sandwiches, pastries and light bites. 🅐 Royal Island, Baa Atoll 🅣 660 0088 🅦 www.royal-island.com 🅔 info@royal-island.com 🅛 24 hours

AFTER DARK

Restaurants
Ayurveda Restaurant ££ ❸ Definitely one for the health and wellbeing minded (it even closes at 21.30 to ensure you get an early night!),

Meedhupparu's Ayurveda Restaurant has a menu based on vatha, pitha and kapha, the three great Ayurvedic life principles. The idea is that you pick the foods most suited to your particular condition or constitution. Choose from South Asian and Western dishes. ⓐ Meedhupparu, Raa Atoll ⓣ 658 7700 ⓦ www.meedhupparu.com ⓒ 07.00–09.30, 12.00–14.30, 19.00–21.30

Dhivehi Restaurant ££ ❹   Advertising itself as the first restaurant in the Maldives to serve only local food, Dhivehi (the name is the word for the Maldivian language) will be of interest to anyone who sees sampling the local fare as an intrinsic part of getting to know a place, or those simply bored of international buffet food. Supplemented from time to time by live music, also local, diners can sit inside in the air-conditioned dining room or outside under the palms. ⓐ Reethi Beach, Baa Atoll ⓣ 660 2626 ⓦ www.reethibeach.com ⓔ info@reethibeach.com.mv

Me Dhuniye £££ ❺   The lunch menu features fusion cuisine snacks and an Asian noodle soup buffet station, while dinner includes both Western and Eastern à la carte dishes, plus a five-course *dégustation* menu, which changes daily. Saturday evening is the big one: a six-course gourmet menu with a different wine to accompany each course. ⓐ Soneva Fushi, Baa Atoll ⓣ 660 0304 ⓦ www.sixsenses.com ⓔ reservations-fushi@sonevaresorts.com ⓒ 12.30–14.30, 19.30–22.30 Wed–Mon, closed Tues

Bars
Meedhupparu ❻   The only resort on Raa Atoll and probably the liveliest resort in the Northern Atolls, which tend to favour serenity over activity, Meedhupparu has a participatory atmosphere, which extends to its bars. Darts, pool and table tennis are there for the energetic, and a disco is held three nights a week, complete with attendant glitter-ball. ⓐ Meedhupparu, Raa Atoll ⓣ 658 7700 ⓦ www.meedhupparu.com

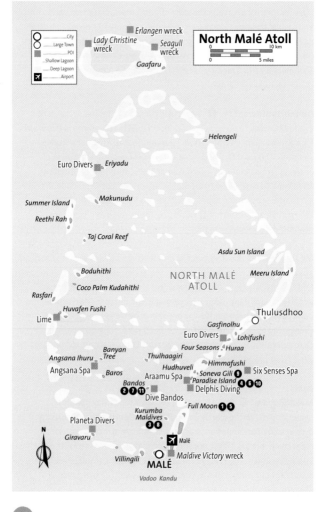

North Malé Atoll

Some 50 km (31 miles) in length, North Malé Atoll is the ring of islands to the north of the capital city of Malé, which is considered a separate administrative area. Thanks to its proximity to the capital, the atoll was the first area in the country to embrace tourism, and today it is home to some of the most famous resorts. It is also the most 'industrial' atoll – although the word must be taken in the loosest, Maldivian sense; don't imagine that any noise or pollution will impinge on your holiday there. Tourists have been visiting since 1972, when Kurumba became the first island hotel to welcome guests, followed shortly afterwards by Bandos. Development continued apace, and the atoll now hosts almost 30 resorts, the majority of which are clustered in its south-eastern quarter.

It would be disingenuous to describe any part of the Maldives as a party zone, but North Malé Atoll is about as lively as it gets. This is due in large part to the fact that airline cabin crews patronise some of the larger resorts that lie closer to the capital on their layovers. The growth of tourism has had knock-on effects for other islands in the atoll. While some traditional fishing islands remain, others have given up that time-honoured pursuit in favour of selling local handicrafts and other knick-knacks to day-tripping tourists.

Burgeoning tourism has also led to the atoll having some of the most established dive sites in the archipelago. Scuba cognoscenti often head for the less crowded northern part of the atoll, where the sites are less frequented and more pristine. The other major diving zone is Vadoo Kandu, the channel that separates the atoll from the South Malé Atoll.

BEACHES

Like the rest of the Maldives, North Malé Atoll offers superb beaches, with little to choose between them. Being so close to the capital, the area does see more boat traffic than most; however, you'll see few signs

⬥ A scenic setting on Paradise Island

SCENIC FLIGHTS

Guests staying on any resort island in North Malé will certainly be conveyed to their hotel by boat, owing to the short travel times and distances involved. While staying in the atoll can be convenient for this very reason, it does mean that you will miss out on a seaplane flight, one of the archipelago's true visual treats. Most resorts offer a scenic flight as part of their activity menu, and it is also possible to book a round trip in one of the aircraft taking guests to the remoter resorts. The downside, of course, is that you will have to pay extra, rather than having it included in the cost of your holiday.

of any pollution. Beaches are invariably pristine, often broad and long, and sometimes surround the entire island. A sprinkling of palm trees on some of them provides a little respite from the heat. Even on the larger resort islands, the beach never feels crowded, as many of the guests will be off diving or in the spa, and you will usually be able to find some space and privacy if you are prepared to walk a little way.

Aside from the resort beaches, the atoll also offers a public beach, on Villingili, the small inhabited island to the west of Malé. Reachable by a short ferry hop from the capital, the beach there, overhung with palms, is popular with local people and independent travellers looking to escape from the resorts.

THINGS TO SEE & DO

Diving

The relatively large number of visitors who come to North Malé Atoll has not compromised the quality of the diving sites. The majority are in the south of the atoll, close to the main cluster of resorts, but there are farther-flung sites in the north. The treacherous conditions of the Maldivian waters are responsible for one of the main diving highlights:

◒ *Scuba divers at Bandos*

wrecks. *The Seagull*, a steamship which sank in 1879 off Gaafaru; *Erlangen*, which met the same fate 15 years later; as well as *Lady Christine* and the unfortunately named *Maldive Victory* of modern times are among the ocean casualties that can be explored by adventurous divers. Thila dives (through long oval reefs or rock formations close to the surface, which channel the current) are also plentiful: Helengeli, south of the resort of the same name; HP Reef, between Girifushi and Himmafushi; Okobe, west of Lankanfushi; and Nassimo, west of Lankanfinolhu, are suitable for divers of various skill levels. Other sites, such as Asdu Rock, south of the resort that shares its name; Hannes Reef and Banana Reef south of the main cluster of resorts in the atoll; plus Hans Hass Place and Lion's Head, at the southernmost rim, offer good snorkelling.

Delphis Diving The amiable and helpful staff at Paradise Island's diving school offer PADI courses for beginners up to instructors. Delphis also has outlets at the other islands run by Villa Hotels.
ⓐ Paradise Island, North Malé Atoll ❶ 664 5243
ⓦ www.delphisdiving.com ⓔ ddcpar@delphis.com.mv

Dive Bandos One of the country's most established dive schools, Dive Bandos even has classrooms for serious scuba students to learn more about the underwater world. A long list of PADI courses can be undertaken, from basic to rescue, adventure and emergency diving. The island also has one of the country's few decompression chambers.
ⓐ Bandos, North Malé Atoll ❶ 664 0088 ⓦ www.bandosmaldives.com
ⓔ info@bandos.com.mv

Euro Divers The Swiss company, which has operations in seven countries, has outlets on several islands in North Malé Atoll, including Full Moon, Kurumba, Club Med Kanifinolhu and Eriyadu, as well as the live-aboard *Atoll Explorer*.
ⓐ H Meerubahuruge, Ameer Ahmed Magum, Malé ❶ 331 6879
ⓦ www.euro-divers.com ⓔ operate@euro-divers.com

◆ The Banyan Tree resort provides five-star comfort

Planeta Divers Various PADI courses are on offer from this helpful diving school.
ⓐ Giravaru, North Malé Atoll ① 664 0440 Ⓦ www.planetadivers.com
ⓔ info@planetadivers.com

Fishing

The one foodstuff of which the Maldives has no shortage is – of course – fish, which also provide another way for tourists to pass the time. If you're after a simple sortie with a hand-line and bait, most resorts can oblige. Serious fishing fans may wish to try game fishing, with sailfish and marlin the largest likely catch; Kuda Huraa, Angsana and Full Moon all offer it. Asdu, Baros, Kurumba and Nakatchafushi have tag and release sport fishing for billfish.

Angsana ① 676 0028 Ⓦ www.angsana.com ⓔ reservations-maldives@velavaru.com
Full Moon ① 664 2010 Ⓦ www.fullmoonmaldives.com
ⓔ sales@fullmoon.com.mv
Kuda Huraa ① 664 4888 Ⓦ www.fourseasons.com/maldiveskh

Spas

The Maldives' lack of any tradition of massage has not stopped its hoteliers spotting another good way to offer even more bliss to tourists. Being among the most advanced resorts in the country, many of the North Malé Atoll islands have installed spa centres, which, depending on the size of the resort, range from just a handful of rooms to larger complexes extending over – and sometimes under – the sea.

Angsana Spa The Thai and Indonesian masseuses at Angsana train for six months in Phuket before being let loose on the island's guests. The eight treatment rooms, including two deluxe ones, come with Jacuzzi and steam room, all of which can accommodate couples.
ⓐ Angsana Ihuru, North Malé Atoll ① 664 3502
Ⓦ www.angsanaspa.com ⓔ maldives@angsana.com ① 08.00–20.00

The hibiscus is used in haircare treatments

Araamu Spa Designed to blend in with the natural elements of the island, Araamu Spa offers treatments and packages of both general massage and the ancient Indian system of healthcare Ayurveda.
ⓐ Paradise Island, North Malé Atoll ☎ 664 0011 Ⓦ www.araamuspa.com
ⓔ paradise@araamuspa.com ⓛ 08.00–20.00

Lime Huvafen Fushi boasts a world first with Lime: the first-ever underwater spa. The facility takes its massages very seriously, outlining its philosophy and treatments in a 40-page communiqué. Whether you're into the theory or not, having your tension eased away while surrounded by the Indian Ocean can't be bad.
ⓐ Huvafen Fushi ☎ 664 4222 Ⓦ www.huvafenfushi.com,
www.limespas.com ⓔ lime@huvafenfushi.com

Six Senses Spa The Thai Six Senses chain has two of the plushest spas in the Maldives. Visiting practitioners, Ayurvedic treatments and wellness activities are among the many services on offer.
ⓐ Soneva Gili, Lankanfushi Island, North Malé Atoll ☎ 664 0304
Ⓦ www.sixsenses.com ⓔ mgr-gili@sixsensesspas.com

Villingili

The fact that the Maldivian government places so many bureaucratic obstacles in the way of independent exploration of the archipelago makes a day-trip to Villingili an appealingly easy way to see something of typical Maldivian life. Easily reachable by a 15-minute ferry ride from the New Harbour (just south of the Indira Gandhi Memorial Hospital), the former resort island has now been converted into Malé's fifth ward and is seeping up some of the capital's surplus residential spill. But its atmosphere is a world away from the frenetic city to its east. The streets of Villingili are quiet and calm, as the residents go languidly about their business. The island does have some sights, an old mosque to the west end of the southern section of beach and a new one at the north-west corner of the proposed stadium (currently a football pitch). There's also a pleasant beach (albeit one that will seem a little mucky by comparison

◓ The old mosque in Villingili

to the constantly raked-over resort ones). But it is mainly suited to simple meandering and enjoying the relaxed vibe.

Watersports

Every resort will offer some form of **snorkelling**; the only difference will be whether this can be done independently from the island or, if the reef is further out, whether an organised boat trip is required.

North Malé Atoll could be said to be the Maldivian **surfing** capital. The atoll has several good surf sites, most of which are in and around the main drag of resort islands. The one thing that keeps tourists away from the Maldives in low season – the risk of squally weather – is the surfer's boon. Peak surf season is from the end of February to around the middle of November, with March to May and September to November bringing the best waves. This timing allows the surfing fraternity to take advantage of the lower prices charged by resorts. During this period waves can reach 2 m (6½ ft) in height.

The main surfing resorts, due to their proximity to the major surf spots, are Dhonveli and Lohifushi, with the former generally held to be the best in the country. Reethi Rah is also recommended by surfers, and Full Moon and Paradise Island attract a lot of wave seekers too. Serious surfers may prefer a specialised charter.

Sun Travels and Tours offers special surfing holiday packages.
🕿 332 5977 🖰 www.sunholidays.com

TAKING A BREAK

Cafés
Sand Coast Café ££ ❶ Serving everything from drinks, snacks and homemade ice cream to main meals, the relaxed Sand Coast Café has outdoor tables on its wooden deck, or you can eat inside under a thatched roof. Enjoy the lagoon view while you eat.
ⓐ Full Moon, North Malé Atoll 🕿 664 2010
🖰 www.fullmoonmaldives.com ⓔ sales@fullmoon.com.mv

○ The restaurant at Angsana Spa

Sea Breeze Café ££ ② Serving a wide range of international staples – pizza, pasta, curries and hamburgers – around the clock, the relatively new Sea Breeze Café enjoys a decent spot overlooking the lagoon, and has an over-water deck from where to take in the view. ⓐ Bandos, North Malé Atoll 🅣 664 3877 🅛 24 hours

Neptune Coffee Shop £££ ③ The poolside café at Kurumba caters for every meal from breakfast to late-night munchies. The snacks and light bites on offer include pasta, sandwiches and burgers and from 11.30 to 16.30 you can order pizza. There's also a selection of coffees and a children's menu. ⓐ Kurumba, North Malé Atoll 🅣 664 2324 ext. 8366 🅦 www.kurumba.com ⓔ reservations@kurumba.com 🅛 09.00–01.00

AFTER DARK

Restaurants
Al Tramonto ££ ④ Paradise Island's highly reputed Italian eatery enjoys a great location on stilts at the end of the jetty, looking out to sea. Theoretically, it is possible to pop in from Malé and dine here, but the logistics and cost of doing so represent a significant barrier. ⓐ Paradise Island, North Malé Atoll 🅣 664 0011 🅛 11.00–23.00

Casa Luna ££ ⑤ Full Moon's swanky Mediterranean restaurant requires you to dress up. Prominent on the menu, which features both traditional and contemporary options, is a selection of fresh fish. Pasta and salads are also good, and you can wash it all down with one of the many international wines available. ⓐ Full Moon, North Malé Atoll 🅣 664 2010 🅦 www.fullmoonmaldives.com ⓔ sales@fullmoon.com.mv

Fukuya Teppanyaki ££ ⑥ Excellent Japanese restaurant next to the buffet hall on Paradise Island. Regular theme nights, such as sushi and seafood, are held, and it is sometimes possible to take your meal at a table on the sand. ⓐ Paradise Island, North Malé Atoll 🅣 664 0011

○ *Dine on the deck or under thatched roofs*

The Harbour ££ ❼ Bandos's stylish fine dining restaurant offers a range of seafood, as you would expect, and a choice of homemade Italian pasta dishes and steaks. Named for the harbour it sits by, guests can sit in or outside, as they dine to the strains of the resort's calypso band. Its proximity to Malé means that it should be possible for non-residents to eat here too, but this would require advance arrangement. ⓐ Bandos, North Malé Atoll ⓣ 664 3877 ⓛ 19.00–22.00

Golden Cowry £££ ❽ Top-class Italian restaurant with a wine list to match. ⓐ Kurumba, North Malé Atoll ⓣ 664 2324 ext. 8353 ⓦ www.kurumba.com ⓔ reservations@kurumba.com ⓛ 19.30–22.00 Sun–Fri, closed Sat

Gourmet Cellar £££ ❾ Bon viveurs will enjoy Soneva Gili's *dégustation* dinners in the small Gourmet Cellar: serving just eight covers it represents the height of exclusivity. Diners enjoy a seven-course meal, with each dish paired with a complementary (but not complimentary, unfortunately) wine chosen by the hotel's resident sommelier. ⓐ Soneva Gili, Lankanfushi Island, North Malé Atoll ⓣ 664 0304 ⓦ www.sixsenses.com ⓛ Dinners start at 20.00 and last for two hours, wine tastings at 18.00

Bars
Main Bar ❿ This large, open bar looks out over the sea and the resort swimming pool, with wooden decking that extends along the beach. Depending on what night it is, you can expect live music, a disco, a magic show or crab racing. Perhaps through concern for other guests' comfort, the karaoke takes place in a separate – sealed – room. ⓐ Paradise Island, North Malé Atoll ⓣ 664 0011 ⓛ 24 hours

Sand Bar ⓫ Relaxed beach bar with an entertainment programme of karaoke, live music and discos. When airline cabin crews are out in force, Bandos can get quite lively. ⓐ Bandos, North Malé Atoll ⓣ 664 3877 ⓛ 19.30–late

RESORTS

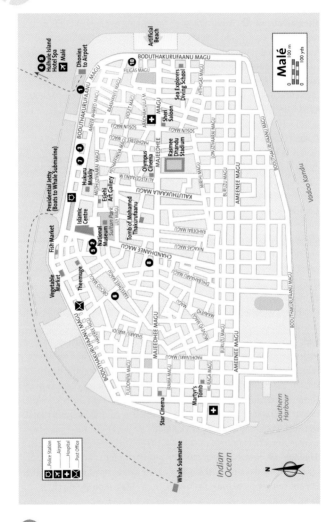

Malé

0   100 m
0   100 yds

BODUTHAKURUFAANU MAGU

Artificial Beach

Sea Explorers Diving School

FILIGAS MAGU

Dhonies to Airport

Hulhule Island Hotel Spa

Malé

Sheri Saloon

Olympus Cinema

Rasmee Dhandu Stadium

Presidential Jetty (Boats to Whale Submarine)

Hukuru Miskiiy

Esjehi Art Gallery

Islamic Centre

Sultan Park

National Museum

Tomb of Mohamed Thakurufaanu

Fish Market

Vegetable Market

Theemuge

Star Cinema

Martyr's Tomb

KALUTHUKKAALA MAGU

CHANDHANEE MAGU

MAJEEDHEE MAGU

BODUTHAKURUFAANU MAGU

AMEENEE MAGU

Vadoo Kandu

Southern Harbour

Whale Submarine

Indian Ocean

N

Police Station
Airport
Hospital
Post Office

38

Malé

As capital cities go, Malé is about as different from the rest of the country as it gets. While the other islands are serene, with plenty of space, one-storey buildings and a calm interrupted only by the occasional speed-boat engine, Malé is a bustling metropolis, alive with noise, amiable Asian chaos, traffic and office blocks. Of course, compared with most other cities in the Indian subcontinent, negotiating the Maldivian capital is a walk in the park. But if you've spent the past few days on a tranquil resort island, Malé is likely to give you a bit of a culture shock. One of the most crowded cities on the planet, it is home to a third of the country's population. Tall tower blocks soar into the sky and the streets hum with motorbikes, cars and trucks. The coral structures of old have now almost entirely given way to modernity.

But while many Maldivians are not overly enamoured with their capital, it's definitely worth spending some time there, both as a counterpoint to the professional, slick atmosphere of the resort islands, and as a way of experiencing authentic local culture. Malé is the best chance you'll get to see ordinary people going about their daily business, in markets, cafés and parks.

It also has its fair share of sights, attractions and activities. While you won't find world-famous buildings and landmarks, the places of note – which are all within easy walking distance of each other – paint an interesting picture of the country's culture and history. The museum is certainly worth a couple of hours of your time, and there are plenty of pleasant places for a stroll or a sit-down. Quaint cafés offer respite from the constant heat.

Malé is easily navigable thanks to its size. It's difficult to get too lost, as whichever way you walk you'll reach azure sea before too long. The island is bisected by two large thoroughfares, Chandhanee Magu, the main shopping street which goes from north to south, and the east–west running Majeedhee Magu. Most points of interest lie north of the latter, in the area emanating from the presidential jetty, close to where most visitors coming for a day-trip will pitch up.

BEACHES

In contrast to the rest of the country, blessed with postcard-perfect
stretches of golden sand, Malé did not have a beach at all until 1998,
when the government built an artificial one on the east side of the
island. While it cannot compare to the archipelago's typical beaches,
the popularity of the area among Maléans makes it a good place for
strolling and people-watching. In everyday use for sport and swimming,
special occasions see the artificial beach host music shows, parades
and carnivals.

THINGS TO SEE & DO

Diving & watersports

While the main watersports action takes places in the resorts and from
the live-aboard boats rather than out of the capital, Malé is a good base
from which to arrange your aquatic pursuits, as several of the local
watersports firms have their head office here. Many visitors find
organising their diving from here better value than doing so from a
resort island, where you are effectively a captive audience.

Sea Explorers Diving School was the first diving school to come to
Malé and is a good port of call if you want to head out to sea on a live-
aboard for some full-on underwater action. It can also arrange visits to
some of the best dive sites in the area.

ⓐ 1st floor H. Asfaam, Bodufungadhu Magu ⓣ 331 6172
ⓦ www.seamaldives.com.mv ⓔ info@seamaldives.com.mv

Esjehi Art Gallery

One of the oldest buildings in Malé (it was built in the 1870s), Esjehi Art
Gallery was once the home of a nobleman, which is evident in the classy
wooden interior with its panels and carvings. The small gallery displays
local art, which is also for sale. Temporary exhibitions are hosted here,
but even if there's nothing on at the time of your visit, the on-site
workshop means that you'll often find artists around willing to fill you in

◆ *The Grand Friday mosque and waterfront*

on the local arts scene. The pleasant café also makes a nice spot for some refreshment.

ⓐ Medhuziyaarai Magu, east of Sultan Park ⓣ 332 0288 ⓛ 08.00–18.30 Sat–Thur, 14.00–19.00 Fri ⓘ Admission charge

Football

Rasmee Dhandu Stadium The Maldives may not be particularly well known for its football, but it's the biggest sport in the archipelago and a popular way for islanders to pass the time. The national side's greatest achievement on the world stage was a 0–0 draw at home to South Korea after reaching the second stage of Asian qualifying for the 2006 World Cup. The 12,000-capacity national stadium hosts local league matches, as well as international fixtures. It's also used for other sports. There is no online or telephone booking system; simply go along if you find out that a fixture is scheduled.

ⓐ Between Majeedhee Magu and Mirihi Magu

Islamic Centre

The closest thing that the Maldives has to a recognisable monument, the golden dome of the Grand Friday mosque and bright white Islamic Centre can be seen from all around the city. It is most impressive for its size – the prayer hall has a capacity of 5,000 worshippers. Inside, the place is decorated with large chandeliers and marble, and with Arabic signage and wood carvings.

○ *The Islamic Centre dominates the skyline*

ⓐ Between Medhuziyaarai Magu and Ameer Ahmed Magu
🕐 09.00–17.00, except during prayer times

Markets

Malé's **fish market** is a lively place, showcasing the Maldives' main industry outside tourism. Not for the faint-hearted, you'll see your fair share of blood and guts and sensitive noses may not appreciate the olfactory environment. But there's plenty of activity to admire. Watching fishmongers reducing a discernible fish to slices of meat in a matter of seconds and a few deft flicks of the knife is one highlight; the huge eels laid out in the middle of the floor are another. The busiest time is the afternoon.

ⓐ Between Boduthakurufaanu Magu and Haveeree Higu 🕐 Around 06.00–21.00

More laidback than the fish market, the **vegetable** or **local market** has a range of good produce and more. Traders from all over the archipelago arrive here to offload their goods, from traditional handicrafts to modern

clothes. There is nothing like the hard sell you'd be subjected to elsewhere in the Indian subcontinent, and the market is a pleasant place for hassle-free browsing and chatting with the market traders.
ⓐ Between Boduthakurufaanu Magu and Haveree Higu

National Museum

This absorbing museum charts the islands' history from Buddhist times through the country's centuries as a sultanate to the modern-day Maldives. Sultanic accoutrements are among the most striking items, with thrones, regal costumes and a palanquin offering a fascinating insight into the sovereign lifestyle. Quirky exhibits from other points in the archipelago's history – including a Maldivian flag that has been to the moon, and the motorbikes used in an attempted coup (replete with bullet holes) – add to the colour. The museum is housed in a three-level colonial building that was once the Sultan's Palace.
ⓐ Sultan Park ❶ 332 2254 ❶ Sat–Thur 09.00–15.00, closed Fri and public holidays ❶ Admission charge

Olympus Cinema

If you don't mind the shaky, grainy delivery, you can take in a film at the state-run cinema, the oldest functioning one in the country. The programme is usually a Hollywood or Bollywood effort, but the venue also plays hosts to sporadic foreign film festivals and other special events. Occasional local productions are also shown. You're unlikely to pay much more than $2.
ⓐ Majeedhee Magu, opposite the National Stadium

Spas, fitness & relaxation

Hulhule Island Hotel Spa Ideal for winding down before or after your flight, the airport hotel spa opened its doors in 2007. With staff brought in especially from the Philippines, the pristine facility features a Jacuzzi, sauna and steam room and couples' treatment room.
ⓐ Hulhule Island Hotel, Hulhule Island ❶ 333 0888 ⓦ www.hih.com.mv
ⓔ sales@hih.com.mv

Sheri Saloon Women only spa/gym/health centre offering yoga, fitness, aerobics classes and massage, as well as a range of health and beauty products to buy.

ⓐ H Rab'ee Manzil, Sosun Magu ❶ 331 0310 ⓔ sheri@dhivehinet.net.mv

Sultan Park

The former grounds of the Sultan's Palace, in which the National Museum is located, are the oldest part of the complex, dating as far back as the 17th century. Today it's popular with the country's migrant workers as well as tourist groups, particularly on Friday afternoons. Charming tropical plant displays make the park a pretty spot for a rest. Outside the park's imposing wrought-iron gates is the republican monument Jumhooree Binaa, a contemporary statue that stands in contrast to the historical park and palace.

ⓐ Between Medhuziyaarai Magu, Chandhanee Magu and Lily Magu.
🕒 Sat–Thur 08.00–18.00, Fri 16.00–18.00

Theemuge

Blue and white in design, the Presidential Palace is a new building, and more impressive than Mulee-Aage, which it has replaced as the leader's seat of power. Visitors aren't allowed in, but it can be viewed and photographed from the outside. The brainchild of an architect from Malaysia, Theemuge is an unusual combination of local and modern styles.

ⓐ Orchid Magu

Whale Submarine

Anyone keen on experiencing the Maldives' sub-aquatic world without having to get wet can take a submarine ride down into the deep – 36.5 m (120 ft) down onto the seabed to be precise. On a sortie that lasts three-quarters of an hour, the German-built sub makes one stop en route to the bottom of the sea.

❶ 333 3939 ⓦ www.submarinesmaldives.com.mv
ⓔ tsub@dhivehinet.net.mv

TAKING A BREAK

Cafés

Malé café life comes mostly in the form of tea shops, small places that open as early as 05.00 and close as late as 01.00, sometimes even later during Ramadan (when they close during the day).

Queen of the Night £ ❶ Despite the suggestive name, Queen of the Night is a tea shop rather than a nightspot. A friendly place near the airport ferry jetty, it serves up bargain Maldivian short eats such as spicy fishcake and deep-fried fish rissole, all washed down with copious amounts of tea. Outside, Malé customers play board games, giving the café a relaxed, olde-worlde feel. ⓐ Boduthakurufaanu Magu, close to the airport ferry

Seagull Café £ ❷ Laidback and casual, sandy-floored Seagull Café has a charming covered garden, and customers are kept cool with fans. The menu has elements of Asian, European and American cuisine, with a good range of sandwiches, snacks, milkshakes, teas and juices. Best of all are the Italian ice creams. All of this ensures Seagull's perennial popularity. ⓐ Fareedhee Magu ❶ 332 3792

Shell Beans £ ❸ As well as great coffee, the fresh bread and cakes supplied by the bakery at Bandos are the chief draws at this amiable little seafront café. Pastries, sandwiches, snacks and desserts are also good; this place does a roaring trade with tourists and expats, although the prices are remarkably reasonable.
ⓐ Boduthakurufaanu Magu ❶ 333 3686

Faru Coffee House ££ ❹ Part of the airport hotel on Hulhule Island, a short hop from Malé proper, Faru is a relaxing place to recuperate from or prepare for a long flight. Brightly decorated with comfortable wicker furniture, it looks out over the hotel's garden. The menu spans Far Eastern, Asian, European and Italian cuisines. Though expensive by Malé

● *The colourful streets of Malé*

standards, the food and service are of international quality and nothing costs more than $20. ⓐ Hulhule Island Hotel, Hulhule Island ⓣ 333 0888 ⓦ www.hih.com.mv ⓔ sales@hih.com.mv ⓛ 24 hours

AFTER DARK

Restaurants

As well as offering visitors a chance to sample the native cuisine away from the resorts' somewhat sanitised version, the capital's restaurants serve up Far Eastern, Indian, Italian and grill-style dishes. You won't be able to get any alcohol (although some places stock non-alcoholic beer as a substitute); coffee machines have sprung up to fill the gap. Many ingredients are imported, which obviously pushes up the price. Restaurants in Malé usually close around 23.00. Bear in mind that they will also be closed throughout the month of Ramadan.

Olive Garden £ ⑤ Day-trippers and Maldivians alike flock to this Mediterranean eatery, which has helpful staff and has been nicely done out with plants and pictures on the walls. Good value and varied food and the cool temperature both recommend the restaurant. ⓐ Fareedhee Magu ⓣ 331 2231 ⓔ capla@dhivehinet.net.mv

Salsa Royal £ ⑥ The erstwhile Twin Peaks, this place is among Malé's best-known eateries. The main themes are Italian and Thai, and it does a good line in pizza. Well air-conditioned and non-smoking, spick and span Salsa Royal offers decent-sized portions and efficient service. ⓐ Orchid Magu ⓣ 332 7830

Thai Wok £ ⑦ A Thai trailblazer on the local scene, the restaurant varies from packed to empty. What does not vary is the excellent food, which rates highly for both ethnic authenticity and portion size. On busier nights getting served can take a while, but the smartly dressed waiters are always friendly. Despite its quality and reputation, the food remains great value. ⓐ Ameer Ahmed Magu ⓣ 331 0007

Symphony Restaurant ££ ❾ Malé stalwart Symphony offers a smart and stylish ambience, with low-level lighting and vigorous air-conditioning. Part of an alliterative trilogy, its sister eateries are the high-class Symphonic, housed in the Maagiri Tourist Lodge Hotel on Boduthakurufaanu Magu, and the bright and cheerful Synthiana on Ameenee Magu. Both the seafood and Indian dishes on the wide-ranging menu get rave reviews. ⓐ Athamaa Goalhi, off Majeedhee Magu ☎ 332 6277

Bars

Champs Bar ❾ An oasis for alcohol fans, Champs Bar has been designed in the style of an American sports bar. Pool, darts and table football vie with the on-screen sport for your attention. ⓐ Hulhule Island Hotel, Hulhule Island ☎ 333 0888 ⓦ www.hih.com.mv ⓔ sales@hih.com.mv ⓛ 16.00–01.00

Live music

Red Zanzibar £ ❿ Rated by many as one of the city's top eateries, Red Zanzibar hosts live jazz in the evening from time to time. Its open-air design, views over the artificial beach, plush décor and impressive menu make this one of Malé's trendiest venues. There's even free internet access downstairs. The absence of any clubs proper only strengthens its appeal. ⓐ Boduthakurufaanu Magu, opposite the artificial beach ☎ 334 0951

Ari Atoll

One of the largest atolls in the Maldives, Ari measures 80 km by 30 km
(50 miles by 19 miles), and is about the same size as North and South
Malé atolls put together. Located to the west of South Malé Atoll, it saw
the third wave of resort building in the early 1990s, following on from
the two atolls either side of the capital, which were developed two
decades earlier. With around 30 resort islands at the moment, Ari has
the most number of islands given over to tourism.

The pursuit of the tourist dollar has edged out many of the more
traditional island pastimes, such as fishing, turtle hunting and coral
gathering, as atoll residents seek employment in resorts, or in auxiliary
industries such as making the handicrafts that supply the holiday
souvenir market. One old way of life that does continue in the atoll is
shark hunting. And it is the presence of sharks that serves as one of the
main attractions for scuba divers; whale sharks are particularly common
visitors to the area. The atoll is also rated highly for thila diving.

Ari's resorts have a similar formation to those in North Malé Atoll,
with the largest cluster gathered in the south-east corner of the ring.
In administrative terms, Ari also includes tiny Thoddoo Atoll and Rasdhoo
Atoll. The latter, which lies to the north-east of the main ring of islands,
is home to Kuramathi, unique in the country for having three separate
(but associated) resorts on one long island, making it a good choice for
anyone who fears they might get island fever. The Hilton, meanwhile,
has gone the other way: its one hotel, which was recently rebranded
as Conrad Maldives Rangali Island, is spread over two islands, Rangali
and Rangalifinolhu.

BEACHES

Ari has the usual selection of fantastic beaches, and it is almost
impossible to deem one any better than the others. If you're seeking an
alternative to the usual stretch of sand, some resorts, such as Sun Island
at the southern tip of the atoll, have village (inhabited) islands in their

The fittingly named Sun Island

vicinity, and boat their guests over there to give them a change of scenery. Another option is to head for picnic islands, like Gaathufushi, somewhere near the middle of the northern half of Ari, close to Fesdu resort. These are technically uninhabited islands, usually colonised by a resort and given basic facilities such as bathroom, showers and café. Although few Maldivian beaches can be improved upon, picnic islands do have a natural, rough-hewn charm that can make an appealing change from the landscaped, constantly raked sands of the resorts.

THINGS TO SEE & DO

Boat trips

A variety of boat trips are available from most resorts, from one-hour sunset cruises at dusk, fishing outings and dolphin-spotting, to day-long excursions that take in a village island (albeit one that is very geared up for tourists), picnic island and usually another resort.

UP, UP & AWAY

Ari Atoll's moderate distance from the capital Malé means that guests may be brought to their resort by either seaplane or speed boat. While the plane journey will be between 15 and 35 minutes, going by boat can take in the region of two hours. If you've been allocated a speed-boat transfer and would rather enjoy the scenic (and potentially smoother) flight, it is usually possible to purchase an upgrade when you arrive at Malé Airport.

If you're keen on spending a bit more time at sea, there are a couple of options. One is a live-aboard. The *Atoll Explorer*, the most famous name in the game, has two routes starting from Malé, one of which is to Ari Atoll. A former oilrig supply ship, the boat now contains 20 air-conditioned cabins with private bathroom. There's even a Jacuzzi. Live-aboards, or safaris as they are sometimes known, often appeal in particular to divers, as they can reach the remoter, less-traversed dive sites; the *Atoll Explorer* has an on-board PADI dive centre, run by Euro Divers.

ⓐ Universal Enterprises Pvt Ltd, 39 Orchid Magu, Malé ⓣ 332 2971
ⓔ explorer@dhivehinet.net.mv

Another option for nautical types – provided they are on a generous budget – is Dhoni Mighili, a resort that consists simply of a handful of *dhonies*, the traditional Maldivian fishing vessel, albeit an incredibly upmarket version complete with air-conditioning, mod cons such as LCD television and a dedicated crew and butler. The accommodation itself is actually in the boats, which are moored alongside bungalows on the island. The *dhonies* are at liberty to sail off at any time, and can even make the journey to the airport to collect you. If you have a spare $12,000 knocking around you can reportedly rent the whole island.

ⓐ Dhoni Mighili, Ari Atoll ⓣ 666 0727 ⓦ www.dhonimighili.com
ⓔ info@dhonimighili.com

Diving

Ari is lacking the long stretches of barrier reef that can be found elsewhere in the archipelago; its reef has many passages and a huge diversity of marine life. There are several wrecks: Halaveli diving school has deliberately sunk a 33 m (108 ft) cargo ship for exploration, and the site, a short distance from the reef, is now home to several blotched fantail rays; Mirihi's dive school did the same with a Taiwanese fishing vessel; and an erstwhile fishing trawler north of Viligilee Falhu is another option for wreck dives. There are numerous thila dives to do as well, with Fish Head, or Mushimasmingali Thila, south of the island of the same name, considered among the most rewarding. The 2.5 km (1½ mile) Gangehi Kandu is one of the longest channels in the country. The house reef to the south of Ellaidhoo is held by the diving fraternity to be one of the best in the entire country. The atoll has a decompression chamber on Kuramathi.

Euro Divers The 30-year-old firm runs courses from beginner level up to assistant instructor. Its Ari-based outlets are on White Sands, Velidhu and Vilamendhoo; the head office itself is in the capital.
ⓐ H Meerubahuruge, Ameer Ahmed Magu, Malé ⓣ 331 3868
ⓦ www.euro-divers.com ⓔ regional-maldives@euro-divers.com

Ocean Pro Dive School A Swiss company, Ocean Pro has three branches in Ari Atoll, at Veligandu, Lily Beach and Mirihi. Services include early morning, two-tank and night dives as well as free Nitrox.
ⓣ 778 1605 ⓦ www.oceanpro-diveteam.com ⓔ mirihi@oceanpro-diveteam.com

Sub Aqua A top diving destination because of its superb house reef, Ellaidhoo's diving operation is run by the German company Sub Aqua. As you'd expect, there is a vast range of courses and services such as Nitrox, Draeger Atlantis 1 SCR and Buddy Inspiration CCR, PADI, NAUI, ANDI and RAB from which to choose. Other great dive sites are also within easy reach.

@ Ellaidhoo, Ari Atoll ☎ 666 0586 Ⓦ www.travelin-maldives.com
@ info@ellaidhoo.com.mv

TGI Diving A Maldivian company that has now expanded overseas, TGI has nearly two decades of experience. Two dives are organised a day, with night dives possible on request. Choose from a variety of PADI courses; the video centre records your underwater exploits for posterity. The firm has call centres in various European countries. Its UK contact number is listed below; the numbers for other countries are listed on its website. Currently closed for renovation, Halaveli is due to reopen in May 2008.
@ Halaveli, Ari Atoll ☎ (020) 7153 2016 Ⓦ www.tgidiving.com
@ info@tgidiving.com

◆ Take your pick of a range of watersports

Spas

Araamu Spa The excellent spa at Sun Island has 21 treatment rooms offering both Ayurveda and European massages. The emphasis here is firmly on nature, with ingredients grown in the island garden being used in the therapies, to supplement a range of Swiss products. The management avoided chopping down any trees to build the spa, so foliage protrudes prettily through the complex.
ⓐ Sun Island, Ari Atoll ⓣ 668 0088 ⓦ www.araamuspa.com
ⓔ sun@araamuspa.com ⓛ 08.00–20.00

Coconut Spa White Sands' beachfront spa is French-owned and staffed by Balinese therapists. A range of packages and treatments based on traditional Asian practices are administered along with natural products. There's also a steam bath and hot and cold whirlpool. Couples can take advantage of dedicated treatment rooms and there is also a private deluxe villa for the purpose.
ⓐ White Sands, Ari Atoll ⓣ 668 0513 ⓦ www.naiade.com
ⓔ resort@maldiveswhitesands.com

Conrad Maldives For the holidaymaker who wants spa treatment without the inconvenience of having to walk anywhere, Conrad Maldives Rangali Island has 21 over-water spa villas, which have adjoining treatment rooms attached. There's also a restaurant in the same complex, whose menu is based on holistic principles. The spa itself is built over the sea too, so you can look down at the fish as you're massaged, before taking a dip in the outdoor Jacuzzi.
ⓐ Conrad Maldives Rangali Island, Ari Atoll ⓣ 668 0629
ⓦ www.hilton.com/worldwideresorts ⓔ maldives@hilton.com

Watersports

Ari Atoll has the usual complement of watersports, including snorkelling, paragliding, canoeing, windsurfing, parasailing, wake boarding, jet-skiing and banana boating. If this is likely to be a big part of your holiday, it's worth checking ahead about the basis on which the sports are provided: some resorts offer non-motorised watersports free of charge.

Watersports Center Sun Island guests can take their pick from jet-skiing, banana boating, fun tubing, knee boarding, sailing, canoeing, speed boating and catamaran sailing. The resort also has plans to purchase some parasailing boats. Aficionados are catered for by the island's own brand, Gaastra, which offers more high-performance equipment, lessons and courses for those who take their watersports seriously.
ⓐ Sun Island, Ari Atoll ⓣ 668 0088 ⓦ www.villahotels.com
ⓔ reservations@sun-island.com.mv ⓛ 09.00–13.00, 14.00–18.00

TAKING A BREAK

Cafés
Lily Beach Coffee Shop ££ ❶ Guests can choose from an à la carte menu, or enjoy snacks, ice cream, tea and coffee by the two pools. Occasional evening entertainment includes live music, a DJ and magic show. ⓐ Lily Beach, Ari Atoll ⓣ 668 0552 ⓦ www.lilybeachmaldives.com
ⓔ info@lilybeachmaldives.com

Vani Coffee Shop and Bar ££ ❷ Partially open-air, with tables extended out onto the beach and below the palm trees, Vani serves a range of international meals and snacks plus tea, coffee and ice cream. Ideal for relaxing over a drink. ⓐ Sun Island, Ari Atoll ⓣ 668 0088
ⓦ www.villahotels.com ⓛ 24 hours

Atoll Market restaurant £££ ❸ Offering a more relaxed environment than some of the island's posher eateries, the sandy floors and lagoon views give Atoll Market a laidback feel. The menu features a range of international cuisines, including sushi, curry, pizza and pasta.
ⓐ Conrad Maldives Rangali Island, Ari Atoll ⓣ 668 0629
ⓦ www.hilton.com/worldwideresorts ⓔ maldives@hilton.com
ⓛ 07.00–22.30

AFTER DARK

Restaurants

Ristorante Al Pontile & Bar ££ ④ Two of the country's most popular cuisines – thanks to the large numbers of guests from the respective countries – are combined in Al Pontile (the name, which means the jetty, gives a clue to its location). The main menu is Italian, as evidenced by the traditional trattoria décor, but a corner has been given over to Japanese dining. You can also get pizza to take away. ⓐ Sun Island, Ari Atoll ⓣ 668 0088 ⓦ www.villahotels.com ⓛ 11.00–23.00

Siam Garden ££ ⑤ This stylish and classy Thai restaurant from Kuramathi Cottage is also open to guests of the other two resorts on the island. Surrounded by greenery, it is done out in dark wood and adorned

▲ *Seafood and sea life at the Ithaa Undersea Restaurant*

with ethnic statues. The food and service are both highly recommended, and the authenticity of the food is ensured by a native staff.
ⓐ Kuramathi, Ari Atoll **ⓣ** 666 0527 **ⓦ** www.kuramathi.com

Ithaa Undersea Restaurant £££ **⓺** Prepare to splash serious cash at another Maldives' first – the world's only all-glass undersea restaurant. Set 5 m (16 ft) below the surface of the sea, Ithaa's extraordinary visual aspect is matched by its contemporary take on Maldivian food – the menu features lobster and caviar among other specialities, washed down with champagne. Smart dress is required, as is well over $200 per person. **ⓐ** Conrad Maldives Rangali Island, Ari Atoll **ⓣ** 668 0629
ⓦ www.hilton.com/worldwideresorts **ⓔ** maldives@hilton.com
ⓛ 18.30–24.00

Bars
Mekenu Bar **⓻** Overlooking the lagoon, Mekenu has an extensive menu of drinks both with alcohol and without, including cocktails and juices. The bar also hosts an occasional programme of evening entertainment. **ⓐ** Sun Island, Ari Atoll **ⓣ** 668 0088
ⓦ www.villahotels.com **ⓛ** 24 hours

Rangali Bar **⓼** Another casual venue from the Hilton resort, with sandy floor and loungers to help you wind down. The bar serves snacks and cocktails, set off with live music and a view over the lagoon.
ⓐ Conrad Maldives Rangali Island, Ari Atoll **ⓣ** 668 0629
ⓦ www.hilton.com/worldwideresorts **ⓔ** maldives@hilton.com
ⓛ 10.00–24.00

POI
Shallow Lagoon
Deep Lagoon

Vadoo Kandu

Dive Centre
Laguna
Laguna Maldives ❶ ❹

Vadoo
Vadoo Diving Club &
Barberyn Ayurveda
Health Centre

Taj Exotica ❺

Bolifushi ❷

Diverland
Embudu

Indian
Ocean

SOUTH MALÉ
ATOLL

Gulhi

Veligandu Huraa

Bodu
Huraa
Dhigufinolhu

Como Shambhala
Maafushi
Cocoa Island

Biyadhoo

Villivaru
Kandooma
Guraidhoo

❻ Club Rannalhi
Rannalhi Dive Shop
& Diving School

❸
Fihalhohi

N

Indian Ocean

Fun Island

Olhuveli Beach

Rihiveli Beach

South Malé Atoll

0   5 km

0   3 miles

South Malé Atoll

Hot on the heels of its northern neighbour, South Malé Atoll saw the second wave of tourism development in the 1970s. It now has just under 20 resorts, most of which are grouped in the southern half of the east side of the atoll, which is 36 km by 19 km (22 miles by 12 miles).

South Malé Atoll is separated from the capital by the Vadoo Kandu, or channel. At 3.6 km (2¼ miles) from one side to the other, it will be a longer transfer from the airport to your resort than it would be were you staying in North Malé Atoll. Conditions are also different from sailing within an atoll, and the sea can be rough at times as you make the crossing. But the choppy channel that is so unappealing to newly landed

⬥ Stunning views from the seaplane

passengers is manna from heaven to divers. They come in their droves, attracted by the kandu diving on offer.

BEACHES

Like all other atolls in the archipelago, the beaches of South Malé Atoll typically boast golden sands, lolling palm trees and azure waters. If you think you may want to escape the resort beach atmosphere, Rihiveli Beach has two uninhabited islands in its large lagoon.

THINGS TO SEE & DO

Diving

The main pull that South Malé Atoll exerts on the diving community is the kandu, or channel, diving it offers. In kandu diving, huge quantities of seawater get flushed through narrow channels, generating exhilarating currents that give divers a roller-coaster ride through the deep. There are three popular sites close to Vadoo Kandu. Vadoo Caves, north of the island of the same name, where the reef descends steeply into the channel, are rich in sea creatures. The drift diving and large marine life such as white-tip sharks, tuna and turtles are among the highlights. Embudu Canyon is a spectacular site north of Embudu Finolhu, while to the east of that island is Embudu Kandu, a protected marine area with strong currents that facilitate an exciting drift dive.

South of Maafushi, Cocoa Corner sees grey and white-tip sharks and eagle rays patrolling the area; the channel here goes down as far as 40 m (131 ft). Beginners are catered for at *Kuda Giri*, a steel wreck sunk deliberately that is largely current free. Parts of the atoll have been designated protected marine areas, at which the potential sub-aquatic activity is restricted. They include Guraidhoo, which means there is some great diving to be done close by, Kandu Medhu Faru, a highly rated dive site for its variety of stunning marine life, and Guraidhoo Corner, a popular site that is ideal for underwater photography. Vaagali Bodu Thila enjoys some striking caves and marine life.

Dive Centre Laguna The doyen of the Maldivian dive scene, Herbert Unger, a prominent instructor with around three decades of diving experience in the archipelago, is one of Dive Centre Laguna's main assets. The highly reputed centre has well-qualified staff and offers the usual gamut of courses and extras.

ⓐ Laguna Maldives, South Malé Atoll ☎ 664 5903
Ⓦ www.lagunamaldives.com

Diverland Its proximity to the Embudu Kandu Marine Area makes Embudu another resort of choice for the diving fraternity. Operational since 1990, the Austrian-run dive school offers PADI courses and Nitrox dives. The school boasts that 35 of the best dive sites in the area are within an hour's boat journey.

ⓐ Embudu, South Malé Atoll ☎ 777 1157 Ⓦ www.diverland.com
Ⓔ info@diverland.com

Rannalhi Dive Shop & Diving School The active dive school at Club Rannalhi runs boat and house-reef diving PADI courses, while the associated shop sells all the aquatic equipment you might need.

ⓐ Club Rannalhi, South Malé Atoll ☎ 664 2688
Ⓦ www.clubrannalhi.com Ⓔ front@rannalhi.com.mv

Vadoo Diving Club In its first incarnation, when it opened in the late 1970s, the resort was known as Vadoo Diving Paradise, and it retains the same draw for divers today, largely thanks to the island's position just south of the Vadoo Channel. Various PADI courses and dives of all levels are on offer. There are five protected marine sites within easy reach and the house reef is also excellent.

ⓐ Vadoo, South Malé Atoll ☎ 664 3976 Ⓦ www.vadoo.net
Ⓔ vadoo@vadoo.com.mv

Spas

Several of the spas in the atoll attempt to provide something more than a simple relaxing massage with calming music playing in the

◆ *Divers' delight: meeting the extraordinary humphead wrasse*

background. Indian concepts such as yoga and Ayurveda, the ancient
system of wellbeing, feature prominently.

Barberyn Ayurveda Health Centre Notably terming itself a health centre
rather than a plain old spa, this place adheres closely to the principles of
Ayurveda. Staffed by Sri Lankans, the attitude taken is a holistic one,
combining Ayurvedic meals, as prepared by the Sri Lankan-trained chefs,
with massage and health treatments. Customers can also undertake
yoga and meditation.
ⓐ Vadoo Island, South Malé Atoll ⓣ 664 3976 ⓦ www.vadoo.net
ⓔ vadoo@vadoo.com.mv

Como Shambhala 'Silent havens for holistic solutions' is the motto at
Como Shambhala, named after the Sanskrit for 'a sacred place of bliss'.
Like Barberyn Ayurveda Health Centre, the philosophy behind the
operation is a holistic one, governing diet, Asian healing therapies
and yoga. Specialists in the last are brought in from time to time to
host week-long retreats. If the serious and scientific side does not
appeal, the spa also has a hydrotherapy pool and treatments designed
for couples.
ⓐ Cocoa Island, South Malé Atoll ⓣ 664 1818
ⓦ www.comoshambhala.bz ⓔ cocoaisland@comoshambhala.bz

Laguna Maldives The highly rated spa at Laguna provides aromatherapy
and Ayurvedic massages as well as beauty treatments. Rather unusually
for Maldivian resort spas, it also offers mahendi decoration, the Indian
body-painting art. More conventionally, there is also a steam room and
a steam plunge pool.
ⓐ Laguna Maldives, South Malé Atoll ⓣ 664 5903
ⓦ www.lagunamaldives.com

Watersports
While South Malé Atoll does not have as many top-class surfing sites as
its northern neighbour, there are still plenty of places to find good waves

Relaxing resorts are easy to find

in season. Aside from that, the standard range of watersports is available at most resorts. As elsewhere, if you're planning to spend a lot of your time in the water, it's worth checking what's available and how much it costs in advance.

TAKING A BREAK

Cafés
Café Laguna ££ ❶ A café by day; a restaurant by night. Daytime customers can choose from a range of multi-cuisine light bites. In the evening the atmosphere changes, and delicacies such as fondue and flambé are on offer. ⓐ Laguna Maldives, South Malé Atoll ⓣ 664 5903 ⓦ www.lagunamaldives.com

Coffee Shop ££ ❷ This over-water bar-cum-coffee shop serves up Western, Far Eastern, Asian and Maldivian food, alongside marvellous ocean views. ⓐ Bolifushi, South Malé Atoll ⓣ 331 7527 ⓦ www.bolifushi.com

AFTER DARK

Restaurants
Fihalhohi Tourist Resort ££ ❸ Bearing in mind the typical maximum holiday length, the chefs at Fihalhohi have instituted a two-week programme of buffet nights showcasing cuisines from the native one to Mexican and Chinese. 'When in Rome' is the name of the Italian buffet, while on '1001 Arabian Nights' you take your pick from a selection of Middle Eastern dishes. Brits hankering for home will appreciate fish and chips night. Don't be deterred by the buffet set-up – the food here gets good reviews. ⓐ Fihalhohi Tourist Resort, South Malé Atoll ⓣ 664 2903 ⓦ www.fihalhohi.net ⓔ fiha@dhivehinet.net.mv

Four Seasons ££ ❹ Not to be confused with the resort of the same name, the Four Seasons here is Laguna Maldives' Italian taverna-style restaurant. The à la carte Mediterranean dishes on offer can be taken with your choice of wine. ⓐ Laguna Maldives, South Malé Atoll ⓣ 664 5903 ⓦ www.lagunamaldives.com

Deep End £££ ❺ Mediterranean-themed restaurant serving seafood, meat, game and vegetarian dishes. Built over the sea, a central circular section has been left open so you can look down directly into the ocean. The restaurant is approached by a torch-lit gangway. If you prefer a greater degree of privacy, it is also possible to take your meal on the beach or in your villa. If you're celebrating a special occasion – or are simply rich – you can wash down your meal with a bottle of wine that breaks the $1,000 barrier. ⓐ Taj Exotica, South Malé Atoll ⓣ 664 2200 ⓦ www.tajhotel.com ⓔ exotica.maldives@tajhotels.com ⓛ 19.30–23.00

Bars

Dhoni Bar ❻ The livelier bar of the two on the island, Club Rannalhi takes pride in describing its Dhoni Bar as award-winning. As the Maldives go, the resort has an active entertainment programme and vibrant, energetic atmosphere, perhaps due to the large contingent of young Italians among the clientele. A good choice if you're after something different from the usual Maldivian tranquillity. ⓐ Adaaran Club Rannalhi, South Malé Atoll ⓣ 664 2688 ⓦ www.adaaran.com ⓔ front@rannalhi.com

Southern Atolls

Considering its proximity to Malé, parts of the Southern Atolls remain relatively underdeveloped in terms of resorts, perhaps because the atolls are not as closely grouped as they are further north. The slow pace of advancement has made the area popular with the safari boats that ply their course around the archipelago seeking solitude and peace for their passengers. Outside tourism, the activity here is similarly laidback, with

⬤ *Spas enhance the relaxed vibe*

SOUTH
MALÉ
ATOLL

Southern Atolls

0 _____ 20 km

0 _____ 10 miles

○Mahibadhoo

Fulidhoo

ARI ATOLL

Alimatha ■ TGI Diving

Maafishivaru

VAAVU
ATOLL

*Fotteyo
Kandu*

Holiday Island

○
Felidhoo

○ ....Large Town
■ ....POI
............Shallow Lagoon
............Deep Lagoon

❷
Filitheyo

FAAFU ATOLL

Nilandhoo ○Magoodhoo

MEEMU
ATOLL

■ Vilu Reef
*Velavaru
Island*

Werner Lau ■ *Medhufushi* ❶

○ Muli

DHAALU ATOLL

Kolhuvaariyaafushi

○Kudahuvadhoo

Buruni

N

Vilufushi

THAA ATOLL

Kalhafahalafushi

islands given over to fishing and farming. Like the Northern Atolls, there are just under ten resorts already operational, with around the same amount of islands again that have been allocated to developers for future projects. From Malé, you will reach your resort by seaplane, on a flight of between 35 and 45 minutes.

BEACHES

Lack of much boat traffic guarantees clean waters, and some go so far as to argue that the beaches of the Southern Atolls are some of the best in the archipelago. Though ranking the numerous shorelines is well-nigh impossible, strolling the sands at Filitheyo or Vilu Reef Resort might well lead you to agree.

THINGS TO SEE & DO

Diving

Directly below South Malé Atoll, Vaavu is home to the longest unbroken section of reef in the country, at 55 km (34 miles) long. It runs from Hurahu Kandu to the southern point of the atoll. The main diving in these parts is kandu drift diving, and there are several good sites, including Vattaru Kandu, a protected marine area and reef break. Thilas (submerged coral reefs) are also popular, and the atoll is also home to Fotteyo, said by many to be among the top dive sites in the country. It is home to an extraordinary range of marine life, and the coral is particularly splendid.

TGI Diving Having started life in the Maldives, TGI has now spread to other diving countries around the world. Sites in the vicinity include Dewana Kandu, a ten-minute boat ride away. Dive excursions depart twice a day to nearby locations; trips to special sites further afield can also be arranged.
ⓐ Alimatha Island, Vaavu Atoll ❶ 670 0575 ⓦ www.tgidiving.com
ⓔ safari@dhivehinet.net.mv

🔺 *A luscious lagoon on Meemu Atoll*

Vilu Reef Thanks to its proximity to a plethora of superb sites, including wrecks, caves and reefs, Vilu Reef is a popular destination for divers.
ⓐ Vilu Reef, Dhaalu Atoll ☎ 676 0011 Ⓦ www.vilureef.com
ⓔ info@vilureef.com.mv

Werner Lau German-owned firm with outlets in Red Sea resorts and Bali as well as in the Maldives. Barakuda (CMAS), SSI and PADI courses are all on offer, and there are around 30 good dive spots nearby, which remain relatively crowd-free. Night dives and underwater cameras are also on the menu.
ⓐ Medhufushi, Meemu Atoll ☎ 672 0026 Ⓦ www.wernerlau.com
ⓔ medhufushi@wernerlau.com

Watersports
All the usual watersports are available in the Southern Atolls, with Alimatha Aquatic, Medhufushi and Vilu Reef among the islands with a particular focus on aquatic leisure.

AFTER DARK

Malaayfaiy ££ ❶ The elegant poolside restaurant, which also overlooks the lagoon, serves both international and Asian food. Highlights include the sushi and sashimi counter, a variety of homemade breads, pastries and jams and an extensive wine list featuring New World vintages.
ⓐ Medhufushi, Meemu Atoll ❶ 672 0026 Ⓦ www.wernerlau.com
ⓔ medhufushi@wernerlau.com

Sunset Restaurant ££ ❷ Filitheyo's à la carte poolside restaurant serves up contemporary, international cuisine, topped off with some excellent desserts, while the bar has a range of drinks including fresh juices, cocktails, Italian coffee and New World wine. The buffet is also of a high standard, with the resort proudly describing it as award-winning.
ⓐ Filitheyo, Faafu Atoll ❶ 331 6131 Ⓦ www.aaa-resortsmaldives.com
ⓔ fili@aaa.com.mv

▲ *Room service with a view*

Far Southern Atolls

The Maldives' Far Southern Atolls, some of which lie south of the equator, are home to a unique island, where local people and tourists are allowed to mingle freely. Equator Village is based on Gan, in Seenu, the southernmost atoll, an island that still bears the legacy of British presence. The UK had two Royal Air Force bases here, the latter winding up in 1976, and its remnants are visible in the English lawns and converted navy barracks.

Another unique thing about this part of the country is that it is possible to travel in a straight line for 17 km (11 miles) without ending up in the water. This is thanks to a British-built causeway linking Gan with the three islands to its north-west, Feydhoo, Maradhoo and the atoll capital Hithadhoo. No permit is needed to visit these other islands, inhabited by local people, which makes Gan and Equator Village the resort of choice for independent travellers, who appreciate the rare chance to see how Maldivians actually live. The relatively low cost of staying at the resort (in Maldives terms, of course) also endears it to more of a backpacker crowd.

For the moment, Gan has a sleepy feel to it, but this could change in the near future. There are plans to expand Gan Airport to allow it to receive charter flights. Its geographical isolation from the rest of the Maldives has produced linguistic, cultural, flora and fauna variation, and Gan certainly offers a very different experience to that on any of the other islands. After many years of being the only island in the far southern group of atolls to host a resort, it is only now starting to see some competition.

BEACHES

By any normal standards, visitors to Gan have access to wonderful postcard-perfect beaches right on their doorstep. That said, if an immaculately maintained stretch of sand is top of your must-have list, you'd probably be better off elsewhere in the archipelago. The joy of Gan

⬥ *Enjoy idyllic beaches on your doorstep*

is the freedom to head off to beaches that are not overseen by resort management, where you share the space with local people. You can swim at Koattey Beach, at the north end of Hithadhoo.

THINGS TO SEE & DO

Diving

Thanks to the almost total absence of tourism development here, marine life has been able to flourish. This makes Seenu Atoll ripe for divers – who of course get to enjoy the sites without hordes of companions. Another big draw is that the atoll has avoided the coral bleaching that blighted so much of the archipelago. Perhaps the most celebrated dive location is the *British Loyalty*, an oil tanker of several thousand tons torpedoed by the Japanese during World War II. Qualified divers are permitted to enter the wreck itself, where a cornucopia of dazzling marine life awaits. The other main point of interest in the area to the scuba community is Shark Point, north-east of Hulhumeedhoo, so named for the prevalence of white-tip and grey reef sharks.

The Austrian-run firm **Diverland** does PADI courses for divers of all levels of ability from entry level to Divemaster. If you're travelling en masse, call ahead to find out about group discounts.
ⓐ Gan, Seenu Atoll ⓣ 777 1157 ⓦ www.diverland.com

Exploring

The rare chance of exploring some Maldivian villages is not to be missed. Head off by bike, on foot or by minibus (Equator Village runs a tour) to the adjoining islands. There you'll find mosques and schools, as well as remnants of the British navy. At the far end of the causeway is the capital Hithadhoo, the liveliest part of the atoll. There are plenty of tea shops in the centre, as well as a stadium where you may be able to catch some sport. Eidhigali Kilhi, a freshwater lake to the north of the island, is good for bird-watching.

❶ *Seaplane provides a fast and convenient means of travel*

EXCURSIONS
Out & about

Out & about

There are clearly far worse places to be than on a tropical island with top-notch accommodation, limitless wonderful food and unfailingly friendly service! Nonetheless, if you are there for a couple of weeks you might well begin to want to explore beyond the comfortable confines of your resort. Getting around the Maldives is by no means simple – at least not if you try to do it under your own steam. But there are several excursions that can be undertaken.

Obviously where you can go will depend entirely on where you are based, so this section outlines the main kinds of trips you can make. These tend to vary little from one resort to the next. The only specific place that could be suggested as an excursion is Malé – and indeed many of the nearby resorts do offer their guests the chance to spend a day in the capital city. While all its sights are bunched close together and can be seen in a couple of hours, to do it justice and get a real feel for the place it is worth staying overnight, to allow you to see how the Maldivians relax when the sun sets and the heat subsides. This could be done by heading off with the daily boat to the capital on one day, booking a hotel in Malé for the night, then returning with the day-trippers the following afternoon. An alternative would be to travel to and from Malé with the boats or seaplane that the resorts send to and from Malé for collecting and dropping off guests at the airport. Malé itself is covered on pages 39–49.

BOAT TRIPS

The other popular excursion in the archipelago is to get away by boat. This can be as brief as a sunset cruise around your resort island to the turning of your entire trip into an excursion by chartering a boat or booking a place on a live-aboard or safari, a vessel on which guests eat and sleep.

Conditions on such excursions depend entirely on your budget. The most basic vessels have bunks divided by curtains rather than separate sleeping quarters, and passengers are expected to pitch in with chores.

A 'village island' store

🔺 *Travel in a traditional* dhoni

Further up the scale are boats such as the *Atoll Explorer*, which boasts air-conditioned cabins and an on-deck Jacuzzi (see page 53). Private vessels are also the accommodation of choice for the super-rich, with various celebrities, business people and oligarchs opting to eschew resort bedrooms and stay on their yachts.

If this is slightly out of your price range, it is also possible to charter a speed boat and crew from your resort for a day. This is likely to cost upwards of $200. A cheaper option may be to try to do the same thing from the jetty in Malé, where competition seems to help to keep the price down somewhat. To slash the price even more, you could instead try chartering a *dhoni*, a traditional Maldivian boat, although this of course will limit the distance you can cover.

If you fancy a taster of the high life and want to give the yacht experience a try, Kuredhu, in Lhaviyani Atoll, has its own vessel, the *Britt*, which has a capacity of ten and can go out for both the day and the night.

⬤ *Seek solitude on an uninhabited island*

UNINHABITED ISLANDS

Paradoxically, uninhabited islands can often be the busiest places you're likely to visit in the Maldives (outside Malé, that is). These islands are often affiliated to a particular resort. Given basic amenities like toilets, showers and a café, they are then used by various hotels, which send their guests there for a picnic, snorkelling and swimming as part of a day's island-hopping. Because several groups descend at the same time, 'uninhabited' can be something of a misnomer.

There are less mass-market options. Some resorts that have an uninhabited island nearby send guests over two at a time, either for a private sandbank dinner or sometimes to stay the night. On Fesdu, in Ari Atoll, guests who overnight on its Robinson Crusoe island are even given a flag to hoist in an emergency.

If money is no object, you can escape to your own island by hiring a resort: Dhoni Mighili and Reethi Rah are both available for exclusive hire to wealthy guests. Meanwhile, Soneva Gili's The Private Reserve is a separate part of the resort only accessible by boat, which can also be rented in full.

VILLAGE ISLANDS

A popular excursion is often to a nearby village island. Some of these places, also called inhabited islands, are very near certain resorts, which have close ties with the village in question and regularly ferry guests back and forth. Where this kind of island is not quite as near, the resort typically offers visits as part of a day of island-hopping, usually also including a stop at an uninhabited, or picnic island (see below).

The village islands to which you might be taken on an organised tour are not the most representative of Maldivian island life. They are well used to groups of tourists traipsing round, and the market you're likely to visit is one that will have sprung up exclusively with tourists in mind, rather than an authentic Maldivian place of trade. But the schools, mosques and homes you'll pass will be genuine enough, and the pleasantly ad hoc villages make a refreshing change from the spick orderliness of resort islands.

Take to two wheels to explore

Anyone prepared to put serious effort in could try to arrange a visit to a 'real' village island, somewhere a bit more off the beaten track. However, as well as the obvious expense (you'd have to charter your own boat as the inter-atoll ferries used by local people are off limits to foreigners), there is a lot of bureaucracy to negotiate. You'll require an Inter Atoll Travel Permit from the Ministry of Atolls Administration in Malé. To get this, your application must be supported by someone who lives on the particular island you want to visit. This pretty much rules out spontaneous exploration. If you're really determined, a travel agent in Malé may be able to help you jump through the bureaucratic hoops.

Food & drink

HOTEL DINING

The majority of tourists in the Maldives are on full-board or half-board deals, so inevitably much of your dining will be based around the restaurant buffet. You'll probably be assigned a table on your first day, and will take your meals there for the duration of your stay. A waiter will be on hand to supply any drinks you might want, but the buffet is typically self-service. Breakfast is usually from 07.30 to 09.30, lunch from 12.30 to 14.00 and dinner from 19.30 to 21.30. This might initially seem restrictive – especially for people who associate holidays with long, luxurious lie-ins – but with nightlife in the Maldives being so low key, there is little reason to stay up late, and getting up for breakfast should not prove too difficult. Bar snacks, sandwiches and cakes are often available throughout the day (and sometimes the night too) should you feel the need for further refreshment, but you're likely to be charged for them.

Forget any preconceptions you might have about the quality of buffet fare; even in the cheaper resorts, the food is generally glorious. With guests having no other option at mealtimes, resorts have to ensure that everybody is well fed and happy. Islamic edicts, such as the ban on pork and alcohol, do not apply to resorts.

The gamut of nationalities who holiday on the islands ensures a wide range of cuisines are represented, from British, Russian, Mediterranean, Middle Eastern, Far Eastern and Indian to local specialities. Everyone is catered for, from the adventurous gourmet to the stickler for his or her native cuisine. The upshot of this is that for every meal there are dozens of tempting choices from all around the world, each prepared and presented with care and panache. A holiday in the Maldives therefore offers a chance to experience not just the local cuisine but food from all over Europe and Asia. While you might assume that islands with fewer guests might offer a smaller spread, such resorts tend to be the more upmarket ones, in which case an impressive range of dishes is guaranteed.

SPECIALITY RESTAURANTS

If you do tire of your hotel buffet and fancy a change of scenery, or if you're not on a full-board deal, you may end up in one of your resort's alternative à la carte restaurants. Excepting the smallest islands, most resorts have at least one speciality restaurant and some offer a choice of several. The themes vary. Italian and Japanese restaurants are well represented, probably because tourists from these countries come to the Maldives in large numbers. Seafood, naturally, is another staple. Such restaurants are by no means cheap, but the food is excellent: it has to be good to persuade guests to opt for it over the buffet meal for which they've already paid. This quality makes it worth splashing out at least once during your trip.

LIVE-ABOARDS

While live-aboards make a great effort to provide their passengers with a decent choice of food, including fresh fruit and vegetables, the limitations of size and logistics will preclude them offering the same range of dishes as are available on land. Live-aboards appeal mostly to divers, for whom food is not the main point of their trip. But if the varied food is likely to be an important element of your holiday, it might be worth sticking to an island resort.

LOCAL CUISINE

Having served as a handy stop-off point for sailors over the centuries, the archipelago's cuisine has the stamp of a range of cultures, including Indian, Sri Lankan, Arabian and Oriental. The geography of the Maldives is the overwhelming influence on the island's cuisine. Fish is found in abundance. Much of it is fresh, but canned tuna is also a common ingredient of dishes. Farm animals, by contrast, are by and large absent, because very few islands can provide the conditions required for raising livestock. Much of what is eaten – including the Asian staple, rice – has to be imported, which is one of the reasons behind the high cost of food and drink. Because the choice of ingredients has been so curtailed, Maldivian cooks have had to use their imaginations to offer any sort of variety. As a result, fish can be cooked and served in any number of ways, including as a soup, paste, cake or in a curry. Curries – one of the few dishes that reminds you of the Maldives' proximity to India and Sri Lanka – are served far milder than in neighbouring countries. There's little in the way of indigenous fruit and vegetables, and what does grow here, such as coconut, bananas, chillies, onion and lime, is used copiously. The local bread, known as *roshi*, is made from a dough of flour, water, oil and salt, cooked on a griddle.

Almost all resorts give their guests the opportunity to try the local food in some form. Larger hotels will include several Maldivian dishes in their buffet every day, while smaller ones often organise a weekly Maldivian theme night, where guests can sample local specialities often accompanied by traditional music. If you're after a more authentic gastronomic experience, then visit the capital and head for one of its many cafés (known as *hotaa*). Prices will be rock bottom and the atmosphere and clientele typically Maldivian, something that you will not find on resort islands.

Maldivians at home take their main meal at around midday, and eat a lighter one in the evenings. This does not apply to resort meals, where you can eat as much or as little as you wish at any time.

DESSERTS, SWEETS AND SNACKS

Popular in Maldivian cuisine are the snacks known as short eats, or *hedhikaa*, served throughout the day in the cafés of Malé (you can choose your own from a glass-topped counter) and, should you be lucky enough to visit one, in local homes. The short eats often consist of a filling caked in pastry. Unsurprisingly, fish often features, and – be warned – some of these snacks can be on the spicy side. Other fillings contain the usual limited range of domestic produce, such as onion, chillies, coconut and tuna, with ginger, honey and lemon grass also making occasional appearances. In resort buffets, a highlight of the dessert tables is the fruit. Fresh melon, mango, papaya, bananas and pineapple are chopped before you and spread out over the table, along with shards of coconut.

DRINKS

The Maldives' ban on alcohol consumption does not extend to holidaymakers on resort islands, and all hotels there have well-stocked bars. The airport hotel and duty-free shops are also exempt from the rule. Cocktail menus are usually extensive, but prices can be fairly hefty, in the region of $6 to $15. Another good option is juices, made from the lovely fresh fruit served at the buffets. The Maldives produces both Coca-Cola and bottled water, using seawater.

VEGETARIAN

The vast range of dishes available in resort buffets ensures that vegetarians too have plenty of choice.

◆ *Cocktail hour is a highlight*

Menu decoder

Menus in the Maldives will always have an English translation (and buffet dishes an English description), and will probably also feature other languages spoken by large numbers of guests. However, any attempt that you make to say something in Dhivehi (the national language) is sure to delight your interlocutor.

POPULAR DISHES

Bajiya Fish, coconut and onions in a pastry coating

Bambukeylu hiti Breadfruit curry

Bondi White, finger-long coconut sticks

Chicken Mussamma Chicken curry with coconut milk

Fihunu mas Barbequed fish basted with chilli paste

Garudhiya Boiled tuna with rice, lemon, onion and chillies

Gulha Pastry balls stuffed with smoked fish or canned tuna, coconut, ginger, chillies, onion and other flavourings

Hedhikaa 'Short eats': snacks, typically containing fish and deep-fried

Keemia Deep-fried fish rolls

Kulhi borkibaa Mildly spicy fishcake

Mas baiy Fried tuna with onions, garlic, herbs, coconut milk and rice

Mas huni (mashuni) Popular breakfast dish consisting of shredded smoked fish with grated coconut, chopped onion and seasoned with lime and chilli

Masroshi Baked *mas huni* wrapped in *roshi* bread

Raa Pungent smelling but sweet toddy

Suji Sweet drink made with semolina, coconut milk, nuts, sultanas and spices

Theluli kavaabu Deep-fried fish rissole

Theluli mas Grilled or fried fish with chillies, garlic and other spices

Zileybee Batter coils in syrup

FOOD STAPLES
Aafalu Apple
Alanaasi Pineapple
Aluvi Potato
Anbu Mango
Asey mirus Black pepper
Bai Cooked rice
Bakari Goat/lamb
Bambukeyo Breadfruit
Baraboa Pumpkin
Bashi Aubergine
Bataru Butter
Bis Egg
Dhon Keyo Banana
Falhoa Papaya
Feyru Guava
Geri Beef
Hakuru Sugar
Juice Juice
Karaa Watermelon
Kattala Sweet Potato
Kiru Milk
Kofee Coffee
Kukulhu Chicken
Lonu Salt
Mas Fish

Mey Bis Kadhuru Grapes
Mirus Chilli
Orangu Orange
Paan Bread
Riha Curry
Sai Tea

AT THE RESTAURANT
Bai Kaa Thashi Plate
Bill genes-dhee faa-nan? Can I have the bill, please?
Dhai Kotta Iloshi Toothpick
Faakhaanaa kobaitha? Where is the toilet, please?
Fen Water
Fen Boa Thashi Glass
Fulhi Bottle
Godi Chair
Haveeru Sai Supper
Hendhunuge Nasthaa Breakfast
Mendhuruge Keun Lunch
Meyzu Table
Reyganduge Keun Dinner
Samsaa Spoon
Thunfushi Napkin
Uoo Fork
Valhi Knife

Shopping

Unfortunately for keen shoppers, the Maldives has nothing like the plethora of bright and quirky bargains that you'd find in nearby India. The constraints imposed by the archipelago's geographical conditions mean that very little can be made easily, and many of the items on sale in souvenir shops have been imported. On top of that, the Maldivian government's desire to prevent too much intermingling between locals and tourists places another obstacle in front of the indigenous merchandise industry.

HANDICRAFTS

It's not all bad news, though. There is a lively handicraft scene on the islands – the tough part is getting access to it. One option is visiting a village island, which is most readily done as part of an island-hopping day-trip organised by your resort. On the islands there is plenty of opportunity for shopping; indeed, that is one of the main reasons the islanders welcome tour parties. As well as the usual local market fare, such as brightly coloured clothes, sunglasses and a few items that the ethical traveller would be in no hurry to take home, such as shark jaws, you can pick up some decent woodcraft. There is also the possibility, if you encounter a Maldivian at work, of negotiating directly for something made for the home.

The items that islanders make, but rarely have the chance to sell to foreigners, tend to be practical. Villagers have had to be resourceful and have traditionally used whatever was at hand. Mat weaving is one of their skills: mats are typically fashioned out of coconut and other leaves and reeds. The same materials and techniques are often visible in resorts that are trying to maintain a natural vibe. Lacquer work, where a decorative varnish is applied to treated wood, is another popular Maldivian craft, examples of which can sometimes be found in tourist souvenir shops.

RESORT SHOPPING

In general, resort shops can be on the uninspiring side. The items on offer are often the standard souvenirs – mugs, magnets and T-shirts – that could have been made anywhere and have no link with the destination other than to have its name emblazoned on them. You can find a few better choices; many shops stock the set of 'Common Fishes of the Maldives' posters, and the country's stunning scenery means there

🔺 Resort shops such as Angsana offer excellent items

are beautiful photography calendars to be found. There are some honourable exceptions to the general lack of exciting shopping, though. Some resorts, such as Angsana, have gone to great lengths to provide delightful upscale boutiques, full of high-quality products, from candles and incense to gorgeous furniture, drums and dresses. But, as elsewhere, the majority of it comes from outside the Maldives. Meedhupparu is another resort island that has tried to offer its guests a larger range than the usual retail options. But shopping is not likely to be a significant part of your Maldivian holiday.

MALÉ MARKETS

If you are happy to pursue the shopping experience rather than the actual acquisition of goods, then you'll have a much better time. Head for Malé. The town has two main markets, one selling only fish, and the other mostly vegetables (see page 43). The latter is sometimes known as the local market. Both are lively, bustling places, brimming with noise and activity. There's none of the hard sell that you'd have to put up with somewhere like India; the fishmongers know that a foreign tourist has little use for a swordfish, and while the vegetable sellers might try to convince you to buy something, they won't persist if you're not interested. The two markets are charming mainly because they provide rare glimpses of Maldivians going about their day-to-day business.

MALÉ SHOPS

The capital's other main shopping area is Chandhanee Magu, a main north–south thoroughfare that starts a little to the west of the Presidential Jetty. Stores on this street sell electronics, clothes, holiday souvenirs, diving equipment, jewellery, watches and books (including some rare ones). Some of the prices are very competitive. It's also another good place for a wander, to take in the atmosphere. Orchid Magu, which branches south-west from Chandhanee Magu, is home to the STO Shopping Plaza, which houses an impressively well-stocked and reasonably priced supermarket.

◔ Take back some handmade souvenirs

DUTY-FREE

If you're passing through Malé, the duty-free shopping centre at the international airport is well regarded, both for its excellent layout and for its competitive prices. It also offers a rare chance to pick up some alcohol, being exempt from the general ban on selling it. All the usual airport shops can be found, selling clothes, watches, cameras, toys, perfume, food, books and souvenirs. Both credit cards and travellers' cheques are accepted as payment. Goods are priced in US dollars.

BARGAINING

Unlike many of the other countries in the region, there is not really a bargaining culture in the Maldives. Island resort shops are run officially and will have fixed prices. You may have greater luck at more informal places, such as the small shops around Malé, or any village island markets that you may pass through on an island-hopping tour. But the common practice in other countries in the Indian subcontinent of the vendor starting with an astronomical price, negotiating with the seller, and settling on a final sum that is a fraction of the opening offer, is not the Maldivian norm. That said, the one place where it can be worth negotiating – rather atypically – is the duty-free shopping centre in the airport.

Children

The Maldives is not usually at the top of the list of most people's child-friendly holiday destinations. The high cost, the archipelago's reputation as a honeymooners' resort and perhaps a perceived lack of things to keep young tourists entertained all act as deterrents to holidaying parents. But there are plenty of things that recommend the islands for a family holiday.

In a move to preserve their sophisticated, serene atmosphere, some resorts, such as Banyan Tree, have put a ban on children under 12. But where this is not the case, children are welcomed warmly. Professional and friendly Maldivian resort staff will often take time to amuse younger visitors. And while little of the evening entertainment programme in the resorts is aimed squarely at children (the exception is the occasional magic show), some of the events will appeal to children. Crab races, for instance, will entertain younger ones (provided they don't have too developed a concept of animal rights!), while slightly older children and teenagers will get a lot of fun from karaoke and discos. Of course, if you're thinking of taking your children with you, it's essential to pick your resort carefully; if you end up somewhere too sedate you may find yourself with a lot of entertaining to do!

The other main source of fun for youngsters is, of course, the sea. Toddlers and above will derive endless amusement from the beach and splashing around in the sea. And various watersports will appeal to different age groups and levels of courage. Quite young children and weak swimmers can start with snorkelling near the shore. Older, more adventurous ones can go scuba diving (legal from the age of ten) or choose from the other watersports on the menu (with some restrictions). Some scuba courses start off in a swimming pool to break the children in gently. Boat trips (especially if there are fish, dolphins or whales involved) always go down well. And the submarine trip from Malé (☎ 333 3939 ⓦ www.submarinesmaldives.com.mv ⓔ tsub@dhivehinet.net.mv) will also be a favourite.

⬥ *Children will enjoy water-based entertainment*

As Indian Ocean holiday destinations go, the Maldives is wonderfully safe. Upset stomachs are highly unlikely thanks to the exemplary food hygiene and well-known dishes from home. Everyone on your island, guest or employee, is known to the management, which means security is good. Island lagoons ensure generally calm waters and ideal swimming conditions, and you will usually be within shouting distance of a guard. Things to bear in mind are the hot temperatures and general safety in the water.

On the downside, because the Maldives caters largely for couples and divers, you may find that there are few – or no – other children the same age as yours. This makes the friendships that usually form among holidaying youngsters (and the resulting peace that the parents enjoy!) less likely. On top of that, the lack of places to go could be problematic if your children have a low boredom threshold. If you visit Malé, the traffic is not ideal for any child (or indeed adult) without great road sense.

Sports & activities

Organised leisure time in the Maldives falls almost entirely into two camps: watersports, in particular scuba diving, and spa treatments. The former draws committed enthusiasts, who come to the archipelago for the sole purpose of daily (and nightly) dives. The latter also has its devotees, and some resorts offer week-long packages of treatments. But most tourists take up the spa services on a more ad hoc basis, simply as another relaxing indulgence on their big trip.

DIVING & WATERSPORTS

The country's staggering variety of marine life and underwater phenomena, plus its warm, clear waters, make the Maldives one of the top diving destinations in the world. Scuba diving is supplemented with a range of other watersports, although the noisier ones are kept at a distance from the resort beaches to avoid disturbing other guests. If you're serious about your diving, you must choose your resort carefully.

🔺 A number of outlets offer watersports equipment hire

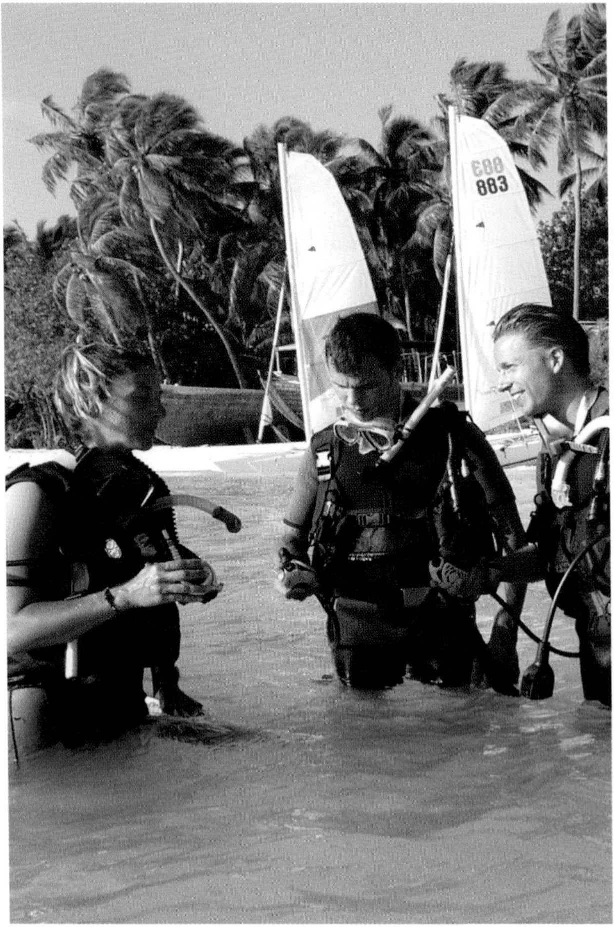

Discover a whole new undersea world

Almost all islands offer some kind of scuba activities, but the facilities vary significantly. At some resorts, the diving is a kind of add-on, just one of a selection of activities. Here, the sites and course you'll have access to will be quite limited – which is fine if you're a novice or casual diver.

Devotees, though, may require something more. The resorts that are most popular among the diving fraternity offer a gamut of courses and qualifications, such as VIT, CMAS, SSI, PADI, NAUI, ANDI and RAB. The provision of extras and safety equipment such as underwater video cameras, Nitrox and a decompression chamber may also influence your choice. So too will the number of dive sites within easy reach of your island. Real aficionados may eschew land altogether and opt for a diving safari, a boat that sails round the archipelago, specifically via the best dive sites.

It may be the most popular, but diving is not the only watersport on offer. A gentler introduction is snorkelling. The equipment can be rented, and some resorts offer courses, although the basics are fairly easy to pick up by yourself. Windsurfing, sailing, canoeing, waterskiing, jet-skiing, catamaran sailing, parasailing are other options. Again, if this is likely to be an integral part of your trip, do your research before opting for a resort.

LAND SPORTS

The other way to pass the time is land sports. Smaller resorts may have just table tennis, mid-sized ones badminton, tennis, squash, a gym and fitness centre, plus a volleyball net on the beach, while a few of the biggies even have their own golf courses.

SPAS

Spas are not quite as ubiquitous as watersports centres and dive schools. Some resorts have them; others are planning to build one. There is no tradition of this kind of therapy in the Maldives, and indeed many resorts import staff from countries with more of a massage culture, such as the Philippines or Thailand. The high quality of services is reflected in the prices, but they are good value compared to their Western equivalents.

LIFESTYLE

Festivals & events

They're not as famous as their Indian counterparts, but Maldivian festivals have a touch of their colour, and allow a famously reserved population the chance to kick back and relax. Some festivals are based on the Islamic calendar, which is lunar and therefore changes from year to year, based upon the appearance of the moon. The following events fall on fixed Western dates:

⬥ A local band plays traditional music

1 January New Year's Day

26–27 July Independence Day
Parades, floats, bright costumes and military marching bands commemorate the Maldives' attainment of full independence from the UK in 1965. The president also makes an annual speech.

3 November Victory Day
Celebrates the defeat of Tamil mercenaries who tried to stage a bloody coup in 1988.

11 November Republic Day
Parades and marches are held to mark the day the Maldives became a republic the second time round, in 1968.

10 December Fisheries Day
Maldivians give thanks for the one foodstuff their archipelago can produce with ease.

The following festivals are based on the Islamic calendar.

1st day of Muharram Islamic New Year's Day

1st day of Rabee-ul Awwal National Day
Street parades commemorate Mohamed Thakurufaanu's vanquishing of the Portuguese in 1573.

12th day of Rabee-ul Awwal Prophet's Birthday
Family and friends gather to feast and celebrate at home.

Ninth month in the Muslim calendar Roadhamas (Ramadan)
The fourth pillar of Islam is taken very seriously in the Maldives. Muslims (which here means everyone) fast during daylight hours. Other pleasurable activities, such as sex and smoking, are also out. Restaurants

close up while office workers down tools early, government officials at 13.30 and private sector employees at 15.00. As usual, the resort islands are exempt from the religious requirements and you need have no fear of the restaurant buffet closing from dawn to dusk! The precise timing of Roadhamas depends upon the sighting of the moon.

End of Roadhamas Kuda Eid (Eid-al-fitr)
Three days of concerts, parades and feasting mark the end of the abstention.

10th day of Zul Hijja Eid-ul Al`h`aa (Eid-al-Addha)
Celebrations and feasting for Maldivians at home, while their travelling counterparts head for Mecca. The local festivities, which include sport, music and dance, last between five days and a week.

Boats are the easiest way of getting around

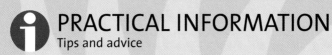

PRACTICAL INFORMATION
Tips and advice

Accommodation

The following hotels are rated on the basis of a double room with breakfast in high season for one night:

£ less than $300   **££** between $300–$600   **£££** above $600

NORTHERN ATOLLS

Royal Island ££ High-quality and eco-friendly resort with classy rooms, excellent food and a serene ambience. Justifiably popular with the rich and famous who appreciate the privacy. ☎ 660 0088 Ⓦ www.royal-island.com ⓔ info@royal-island.com

NORTH MALÉ ATOLL

Paradise Island £ Large, well-run resort whose bar is occasionally enlivened by resident cabin crew. ☎ 664 0011 Ⓦ www.villahotels.com ⓔ info@paradise-island.com.mv

Thulhaagiri £ The unassuming Thulhaagiri is as close to a village as you could get. Excellent food and a beautiful colony of parrots are two of the highlights. ☎ 664 5930 Ⓦ www.thulhaagiri.com ⓔ reserve@thulhaagiri.com.mv

Angsana ££ Funky resort that has eschewed the usual 'natural' aesthetic for bright greens and quirky modern design. Casual and fun. ☎ 664 0326 Ⓦ www.angsana.com ⓔ maldives@angsana.com

Banyan Tree £££ Idyllic retreat with superlative service and beautiful villas with private Jacuzzis. The absence of under-12s and television sets ensures perfect tranquillity. ☎ 664 3147 Ⓦ www.banyantree.com ⓔ maldives@banyantree.com

MALÉ

Hulhule Island Hotel ££ Quality hotel that's ideal if you need to spend the night near the airport due to landing late or leaving early. The spa,

pool, bar and restaurant are all good places to unwind, pre- or post-flight. ⓐ Hulhule Island ☏ 333 0888 Ⓦ www.hih.com.mv
ⓔ sales@hih.com.mv

ARI ATOLL

Angaga ££ Serene resort that is popular with honeymooners. The watersports are good here, and there's a decent entertainment programme. ☏ 666 0510 Ⓦ www.angaga.com.mv
ⓔ angaga@dhivehinet.net.mv

Sun Island ££ The largest resort in the Maldives, guests make their way around the island on bikes and in golf buggies. There are plenty of places to eat and drink and a charming spa. Holiday Island, the sister resort just across the water, attracts a slightly older, calmer crowd. ☏ 668 0088
Ⓦ www.sunislandmaldives.com ⓔ info@sun-island.com.mv

SOUTH MALÉ ATOLL

Laguna Maldives ££ Aesthetically pleasing and elegant resort.
☏ 664 5903 Ⓦ www.universalresorts.com ⓔ lbr@dhivehinet.net.mv

SOUTHERN ATOLLS

Velavaru Island Resort ££ Charming island recently brought under the Angsana umbrella. ☏ 676 0028 Ⓦ www.velavaru.com ⓔ reservations-maldives@velavaru.com

FAR SOUTHERN ATOLLS

Equator Village £ The only place where you share the island with villagers. ☏ 689 8721 Ⓦ www.equatorvillage.com
ⓔ equator@dhivehinet.net.mv

Preparing to go

GETTING THERE

The Maldives is only accessible by plane, and the vast majority of travellers who go there will be on package deals. While it is possible to fly into Malé with a scheduled airline, the high cost of accommodation not booked through a tour operator deters most tourists from doing so. Non-stop charter flights go from Manchester and London, taking between 10 and 13 hours. The main travel agents and some specialist operators offer package deals. Scheduled airlines typically fly between the UK and Malé via their hub: Sri Lankan, Emirates and Qatar Airways go via Colombo, Dubai and Doha respectively. The cost of package holidays varies quite dramatically, depending on the reliability of the sunshine in the Maldives and the weather in the main tourist markets. European winter is peak season.

Many people are aware that air travel emits CO_2, which contributes to climate change. You may be interested in the possibility of lessening the environmental impact of your flight through the charity Climate Care, which offsets your CO_2 by funding environmental projects around the world. Visit ⓦ www.climatecare.org

TRAVEL INSURANCE

Taking out travel insurance is strongly recommended, particularly as you will be spending your holiday on an island, and reaching a hospital in the event of an emergency could be a costly business. It's not likely to set you back much; the most basic packages start from around £1 a day for a two-week break. If you travel frequently, an annual multi-trip policy can work out better value. If you do go for a basic package, you may not be covered for activities such as scuba diving, so bear this in mind before you choose a policy.

TOURISM AUTHORITY

The Maldives Tourism Promotion Board (MTPB) has an office in Malé, whose staff can answer your questions and furnish you with literature about the islands. It has an office in Germany, which responds promptly to emails.

The Maldives Tourism Promotion Board ⓐ 3rd Floor H. Aage, 12, Boduthakurufaanu Magu, Malé ☎ 332 3228 ⓦ www.visitmaldives.com ⓔ mtpb@visitmaldives.com

Maldives Government Tourist Information Office ⓐ Aschaffenburger Strasse, 96g, 63500 Seligenstadt, Germany ☎ 06182 9 934 857 ⓔ info@visitmaldives.de

BEFORE YOU LEAVE

Diphtheria, hepatitis A, polio, tetanus and typhoid inoculations are recommended, though not required, for visiting the Maldives. To be effective they must be taken at least a couple of weeks in advance. The only compulsory vaccination is against yellow fever, if you're arriving from an infected area. Malaria is currently not found on the islands.

You'll need to take any medication with you. While Malé has well-stocked pharmacies, most travellers spend the majority of time on their resort island, where choice is likely to be far more limited. It's also worth taking a good insect repellent and, if you want to save money on your washing, some travel detergent. Suntan lotion, sunhats, snorkelling equipment and other beach paraphernalia can all be bought, but again you won't have much choice so you may prefer to bring your own. A first-aid kit can be useful if you're travelling with children, but resorts are geared up for most emergencies.

ENTRY FORMALITIES

You don't need to organise a visa in advance; all visitors are issued with a 30-day tourist visa without charge. Travellers of all nationalities are required to have a passport that is valid for the duration of the trip, a return ticket and a hotel reservation or enough funds for their stay, defined as $50 per day plus $100.

The Maldives has strict Islamic laws forbidding the purchasing and consumption of alcohol, and these cannot be circumvented by importing your own: it will be confiscated. The same applies to pork products, pornography and, theoretically, iconography of another religion. Reasonable quantities of gifts and tobacco products are allowed. It is an extremely serious offence to bring in any drugs or weapons: penalties can include life imprisonment.

○ A table for two?

MONEY

The local currency is the Rufiyaa, although you could go your whole holiday without seeing a single note. All places that tourists might visit accept US dollars, and resort islands deal entirely in American currency. If you prefer, your whole holiday could be cashless; it is usually possible to charge all purchases to your hotel account and you can then pay by credit card at the end of your trip.

If you do want to change up some cash into local currency, American dollars are best. The Rufiyaa is pegged to the dollar, and the rates for other major currencies are based on that, so there is no need to shop around for a better rate. You will probably have to pay commission of around five per cent on travellers' cheques. Several banks in Malé have ATMs. In the capital, upmarket restaurants and hotels will usually accept credit cards, but smaller places probably won't.

CLIMATE

The Maldives has warm temperatures all year round, varying between 24°C and 33°C (75°F to 91°F). The main climatic differences come from the two monsoon seasons. The winter north-east monsoon, from January to March, is peak holiday season, both for the dry weather it brings and because it coincides with European winter. The south-west monsoon, from May to December, brings wetter weather, although the rain seldom lasts for too long. The rainiest months are May and November; the sunniest is March and the months before and after it.

BAGGAGE ALLOWANCE

Baggage allowances vary from airline to airline and depending on political events, so it's worth checking your airline's website in advance or giving them a call for the latest rules. Your travel agent should also be able to give you an idea. Scheduled airlines tend to have higher allowances than charter flights – typically around 40 kg compared to 20 kg.

During your stay

AIRPORTS

Anyone who has travelled much around the Indian subcontinent will find Malé International Airport a breath of fresh air. Calm and civilised, there is nothing like the usual phalanx of touts, porters and taxi drivers that besiege passengers at other airports in the region. The airport has its own island, Hulhule, a short hop from the capital. When you reach the terminal, you will immediately see two rows of desks which belong to the various resorts and tour operators. Find the appropriate one, and the rep there will give you the details of your airport transfer. If your resort is close by, you'll be going by speed boat. If it's further out, you may be taken there by seaplane. In either case, you'll be given precise instructions, and your airport experience is likely to be orderly and hassle-free. On the way back, your hotel reception will give you the details of your return transfer.

If you're a rare independent traveller, you'll probably be heading to Malé first. Ferries go between the airport island and the capital 24 hours a day, departing the main jetty at Hulhule and jetty 9–10 in Malé. Boats leave every 15 minutes or when they are full, and the cost is Rf 10 or $1. For around five to seven times that cost, depending on the time of day, you can also charter a *dhoni*, a traditional Maldivian vessel that is now usually motorised.

For flight information relating to Malé International Airport, call ☎ 332 2073.

The other kind of airport you may pitch up at is a little more unusual. The seaplanes that convey passengers from Malé to their resorts land in the water before taxiing to a small floating platform, no more than a few metres in length and width. From there, you are collected by boat and delivered to your island. The minuscule nature of the 'airports' can be a source of amusement to the resort companies – one has erected a small sign on the floating platform that reads 'Welcome to Soneva Fushi International Airport'.

COMMUNICATIONS

You'll find payphones in Malé, most of which are card-operated, although some accept coins. Cards can be bought from the head office and outlets of telecom provider Dhiraagu. On resort islands, payphones are usually just for staff use. You can make calls from your room, but these are likely to be fairly costly.

Mobile phone reception is generally good on the islands, but can be patchy when you're out at sea. If all you want to do is exchange a few

TELEPHONING THE MALDIVES
From the UK 00 + 960 + number
From Ireland 00 + 960 + number
From the EU 00 + 960 + number
From the US 011 + 960 + number
From Canada 011 + 960 + number
From Australia 0011 + 960 + number
From New Zealand 00 + 960 + number
From South Africa 091 + 960 + number

The Maldives has no area codes. All numbers are now seven digits long.

TELEPHONING ABROAD
The UK 00 + 44 + number
Ireland 00 + 353 + number
The EU 00 + country code + number
The US 00 + 1 + number
Canada 00 + 1 + number
Australia 00 + 61 + number
New Zealand 00 + 64 + number
South Africa 00 + 27 + number

International operator and directory enquiries 190

⬤ *Local phone booths*

messages with people back home and keep in touch with holiday companions, your mobile phone should suffice.

Postcards and stamps can be bought in your resort shop, and reception staff will send your cards for you. You can also send your mail from Malé. It's Rf 12 to send a letter abroad by airmail and Rf 10 for a postcard. They will generally arrive between three and eight days later.

Internet access can be frustratingly slow and, on your resort island, fairly expensive to boot. Most resorts have cybercafés, although they may have limited opening hours, and access is occasionally possible through the television in your room. Malé also has several internet cafés.

CUSTOMS

The first thing that will hit you when you arrive in your resort is the unfailing friendliness of the Maldivians. Cheerful salutations are routinely exchanged with every staff member you pass. The country's sharia law forbids the consumption of alcohol by the local people. The barman serving your drinks will not be allowed to join you for one. Most resorts will encourage guests to respect the marine life, including the coral.

DRESS CODES

Nudism and topless bathing are prohibited throughout the country. Aside from that, on your resort island dress codes are relaxed, and nobody will object if you walk around in your swimwear. That said, most guests choose to cover up a little for meals and in reception. On Malé and village islands, it's a different story. Modest dress is expected, and you should cover your thighs and shoulders.

ELECTRICITY

The archipelago relies on fuel-powered generators. These are fairly dependable but there may be moments when the electricity cuts out. Output is 220–240 V, at 50 Hz. There is a range of plug sockets, with many hotel rooms having both two-pin continental European and three-pin British sockets.

EMERGENCIES

Ambulance 102
Fire 118
Police 119
Electricity 104
Water 105

If you're taken ill on your island, tell a member of staff. Some resorts have doctors on site; if yours doesn't the employees will help you make the necessary arrangements for treatment. Maldivian resorts are highly professional and should be able to help you deal with minor ailments. A seaplane can be chartered if you need to reach hospital quickly.

The main facilities are centred in Malé. The capital has two main hospitals, one public (Indira Gandhi Memorial Hospital), the other private (ADK Hospital). The latter has doctors on call 24 hours a day as well as a dental surgery and a non-stop pharmacy.

Indira Gandhi Memorial Hospital ⓐ Kanbaa Aisa Rani Hingun ⓣ 331 6647
ADK Hospital ⓐ Sosun Magu ⓣ 331 3553

In the highly unlikely event you need police assistance, alert resort staff. Outside the holiday islands, the police can be reached via the nearest atoll office.

Few countries have embassies proper in the Maldives, but many have some form of representation on the archipelago or elsewhere in the region.

Australia
Australian High Commission in Sri Lanka ⓐ 21 Gregory's Road, Colombo 7 ⓣ (94) (11) 246 3200

Canada
Canadian High Commission in Sri Lanka ⓐ 6 Gregory's Road, Colombo 7 ⓣ (94) (11) 522 6232

New Zealand

Honorary Consul in Malé ⓐ C/- Crown Company Pvt Ltd, 30H Sea Coast, Boduthakurufaanu Magu ⓣ 332 2432

New Zealand High Commission in Singapore ⓐ Ngee Ann City, Tower A, 15-06/10, 391A Orchard Road ⓣ (65) 6235 9966

South Africa

South African High Commission in New Delhi ⓐ B18 Vasant Marg Vasant Vihar ⓣ (91) (11) 2614 9411 ext 19

UK

British Consular Correspondent in Malé ⓐ Dhiraagu, 19 Medhuziyaarai Magu ⓣ 331 1218; British Embassy in Sri Lanka ⓐ 190 Galle Road, Kollupitiya, Colombo 3 ⓣ (94) (11) 243 7336 ext 43

US

American Embassy in Sri Lanka ⓐ 210 Galle Road, Colombo 3 ⓣ (94) (11) 249 8500

GETTING AROUND

Most islands are small enough that they can easily be navigated on foot. The larger resorts provide bicycles or ferry guests around in golf-style buggies. The complications – and costs – begin when you want to leave your island. The Maldives is not geared up for independent travel; in fact it tries its utmost to deter people from attempting it. The government is concerned about the effect that Western visitors' alcohol consumption and insufficient clothing might have on the local population. Thanks to the island geography, it is a relatively uncomplicated task to keep the two groups apart. Bureaucracy, logistics and costs are the main barriers in the way of those tourists who would like to see traditional island life. It is possible to get around them; your best bet is to go to a local travel agent in Malé, which might be able to help you circumvent the obstacles.

Boats

Boats provide the majority of public transport in the Maldives. If you have the money, you can hire a speed boat and crew from your resort or from Malé. Chartering a boat for the day gives you maximum flexibility, but is likely to set you back at least $200. A *dhoni* (a traditional Maldivian sailboat, now usually motorised) is cheaper to hire but slower. Nor is spontaneous island-hopping really feasible. Foreigners are required to get a permit from the Ministry of Atolls Administration in Malé to visit village islands, and even other resorts expect advance warning of a visit and often charge fees for the privilege.

◆ *Speed boats for hire to suit your pocket*

It's easier to make use of your resort's regular boats. Many islands in the vicinity of Malé offer a day-trip to the capital at least a few days per week. Another popular outing is a day-long tour that includes a stop-off at a different resort, shopping and a stroll in a village island, and swimming, sunbathing and a barbecue on a so-called uninhabited island – which can often be rather busy. By taking an organised tour you get round the permit issue. Transport is also arranged to get guests to and from the airport; you can sometimes tag along, usually for a fee, and spend some time in and around Malé. These journeys are scheduled around plane arrivals and departures and are therefore subject to change.

A cheaper option is the ferry. Boats go regularly between Malé and Hulhule airport island to the east and Villingili to the west. It's a relaxing ride and an easy way to see some local life.

Road transport

There is little call for road transport outside the capital, and one of the pleasures of a holiday in the Maldives is not hearing a car's engine for the duration of your trip. The exception, of course, is Malé. The size of the capital might render a taxi unnecessary in terms of distance, but it can be a relief to escape the heat in an air-conditioned cab. Tourists with limited mobility or small children may also appreciate a break from negotiating the city's rather manic traffic as pedestrians. It's also possible to hire a bike or motorbike, although there's little need to do so.

Seaplane

Farther-flung resorts make greater use of seaplanes. It is worth making sure that you take at least one such flight while you're in the country; if you don't get one included as your airport transfer, you can sometimes book a round trip. Resorts often offer brief scenic flights too.

HEALTH, SAFETY & CRIME

Compared to other holiday destinations in the vicinity, the Maldives is wonderfully safe. The food issues of India, say, do not apply here,

◆ *Police officers are on hand to help*

as the resorts have the highest standards of hygiene. Resorts have their own water desalination plants, although most people buy bottled water.

The main health risks come from the hot sun and the sea. Anyone not used to the temperature should drink plenty of fluids, wear cream and a sunhat and head for the shade during the hottest part of the day. While the lagoons around the islands are generally safe for swimmers, and most resorts have lifeguards stationed on the beach, currents can form and patches of the seabed can be sharp. Pay attention to signs indicating safe swimming areas. Divers are advised to be aware of the location of the nearest decompression chamber.

While not in the same league as any Indian city, the frenetic traffic in Malé can still come as something of a shock when you've spent a few days on a serene holiday island. Watch out for motorbikes in particular.

Any healthcare must be paid for. Treatment can be expensive, particularly if you need to be transferred to a hospital. Medical insurance is therefore essential.

Crime levels in the Maldives are very low. Everybody on your resort island is a guest or staff member and therefore known to the management, so theft is highly unlikely. But it's still worth following basic holiday crime prevention rules such as not leaving your valuables unattended on the beach and locking your hotel room. Maldivian police officers are easily recognisable owing to their distinctive hats and blue shirts. They don't enjoy the best reputation in the country, but should come to the aid of a tourist when required.

MEDIA

Your easiest access to English-language media will be through the television in your hotel room. Most have a cable package with international stations such as CNN, BBC World and so on. Local state channel Television Maldives also has some English programmes.

The BBC World Service has now started to broadcast on FM in Malé. Elsewhere on the radio, the government-run Voice of Maldives has news

in English. Several Dhivehi (Maldivian language) newspapers include a few pages of English-language stories.

However, it has to be said that there is not a great range of English-language media available. This seems to be a conscious decision by some resorts to offer a haven where thoughts of the outside world are suspended – summed up in the slogan 'no news, no shoes'.

OPENING HOURS

Business life in the Maldives stops on Friday and often for 15 minutes every prayer time, which takes place five times a day. Shops can open as early as 06.00, although 08.00 or 09.00 is more common. They usually close at 20.00, although some may remain open until 23.00. Government offices and banks are open to the public in the morning, from 07.30 or 08.00 until around 13.30 from Sunday to Thursday.

RELIGION

All Maldivians are obliged by law to be Muslims. The country's strict observance of Islam pervades all aspects of day-to-day life, from the frequent suspension of businesses for prayer time and on the holy day of Friday to the embargo on alcohol. On the resort islands, Islam won't impinge on your holiday at all: restaurants and bars operate seven days a week and you can consume as many cocktails as you wish. But it's worth bearing in mind when in Malé and the village islands that they have a very different atmosphere and expectations from your resort.

TIME DIFFERENCES

The Maldives is five hours ahead of GMT, four ahead of most of mainland Europe. It is 10 hours ahead of EST and 13 ahead of PST, six hours behind Sydney and eight behind Auckland. There is no daylight saving, so the listed times may vary by one hour.

TIPPING

The issue of tipping is nowhere near as prominent as it is in nearby destinations such as India, and does not have a long tradition in the

Maldives. That said, wages are low and the many foreign visitors in the habit of holiday tipping have started to change expectations. Most resorts allocate guests a table on the first night, so you are likely to have the same waiter for most of your stay. If you've opted to have everything charged to your room to avoid dealing with cash throughout your stay, a gratuity can be given on the last day. Some tour companies suggest around $10 a week. There's no need to tip taxi drivers or in cafés. If you ask a local to pose for a photograph, they will not expect any money and may be offended by the gesture.

TOILETS

Toilets on resort islands are uniformly pristine. On Malé they do not look quite as impressive but are still decent. If you're caught short, try asking to use the facilities in a hotel or restaurant.

TRAVELLERS WITH DISABILITIES

Much about the Maldives makes it an ideal destination for disabled travellers looking for a hassle-free holiday on the Indian subcontinent. The main boon is the design of the islands. The charming rule about no building being higher than the tallest palm tree means that the vast majority of facilities are on the ground floor, so you will seldom have to negotiate sets of stairs. Rooms are mostly spacious, easily negotiable in a wheelchair. Professional and eager staff ensure that your needs are met, and will happily shift tables and chairs in the bar, for example, upon request. If you need daily help with aspects of your routine, that can generally be arranged. Should you require ramps – which you may, as hotel rooms sometimes have a step or two at the entrance – contact your resort in advance. Where islands are too large to be easily traversed on foot, a golf buggy service is typically available. Depending on your state of health and mobility, other activities such as snorkelling and boat trips are also possible.

The other main advantage is the absence of cars. Whereas the chaotic traffic in nearby holiday destinations such as India and Sri Lanka can deter even the fully mobile, the serene islands of the Maldives mean you don't have to keep an eye out for any lunatic drivers. Malé, of course, whose traffic could be described as 'Indian-lite', is an exception. Anyone with limited mobility who wants to see the capital city would probably be best off hiring a taxi to do so.

One other slight difficulty that a wheelchair user might face is the ground surface. Many resorts have gone for the 'back to nature' aesthetic in designing and landscaping their islands. While very pretty, the resulting naturalistic paths are not ideal for wheels. But the lack of crowds allows to you to move at your own pace, willing staff will proffer any assistance you might need and you won't feel rushed.

These organisations provide services to travellers with disabilities.

The Royal Association for Disability and Rehabilitation does not respond specifically to queries from individuals, but it does offer some general tips on travel. The website features a news bulletin board on which the editor posts details of overseas travel services. ⓐ 12 City Forum, 250 City Road, London EC1V 8AF ⓣ 020 7250 3222 ⓦ www.radar.org.uk ⓔ radar@radar.org.uk

Tourism for All can provide information packs on some of the top tourist destinations.
ⓐ The Hawkins Suite, Enham Place, Enham Alamein, Andover SP11 6JS
ⓣ 0845 124 9971 ⓔ info@tourismforall.org.uk

Go Maldives, a private travel agent, offers advice to travellers with disabilities and can help you choose the best resort for your requirements. ⓐ 25 Boduthakurufaanu Magu, Malé ⓣ 332 6655 ⓦ www.gomaldives.com ⓔ enquiry@gomaldives.com

FIND THE LATEST HOTSPOT

Get more from your holiday and discover the best restaurants, bars, beaches and family-friendly attractions with these handy pocket guides. Our wide range covers over 45 destinations:

Algarve
Bali
Brazil
Bulgaria:
  Black Sea Resorts
Corfu
Corsica
Costa Blanca
Costa Brava & Costa Dorada
Costa del Sol & Costa de Almeria
Côte D'Azur
Crete
Croatia
Cuba
Cyprus
Dominican Republic
Egypt:
  Red Sea Resorts
Fuerteventura
Gibraltar
Goa
Gran Canaria
Guernsey
Halkidiki
Hawaii
Ibiza
Ionian Islands

Jamaica
Jersey
Kenya:
  Indian Ocean Resorts
Lanzarote
Madeira
Maldives
Mallorca
Malta
Menorca
Mexico
Morocco
Neapolitan Riviera
Orlando
Rhodes & Kos
Santorini
Sardinia
Sicily
Sri Lanka
Tenerife
Thailand
Tunisia
Turkey –
  Aegean Coast
  Lycian Coast
  Mediterranean Coast

Thomas Cook Publishing

ACKNOWLEDGEMENTS

We would like to thank all the photographers, picture libraries and organisations for the loan of the photographs reproduced in this book, to whom copyright in the photographs belongs: Pictures Colour Library pages 64, 89; World Pictures/Photoshot pages 26, 75; all the rest, Vasile Szakacs

Project editor: Penny Isaac
Layout: Donna Pedley
Proofreader: Karolin Thomas
Indexer: Karolin Thomas

**Limerick
County Library**

Send your thoughts to
books@thomascook.com

- **Found a beach bar, peaceful stretch of sand or must-see sight that we don't feature?**
- **Like to tip us off about any information that needs a little updating?**
- **Want to tell us what you love about this handy little guidebook and more importantly how we can make it even handier?**

Then here's your chance to tell all! Send us ideas, discoveries and recommendations today and then look out for your valuable input in the next edition of this title.

Email to the above address or write to:
HotSpots Series Editor, Thomas Cook Publishing, PO Box 227, Coningsby Road, Peterborough PE3 8SB, UK.

HOTSPOTS
MALDIVES

Written by Debbie Stowe. Original photography by Vasile Szakacs

Published by Thomas Cook Publishing
A division of Thomas Cook Tour Operations Limited
Company registration no. 1450464 England
The Thomas Cook Business Park, Unit 9, Coningsby Road,
Peterborough PE3 8SB, United Kingdom
Email: books@thomascook.com, Tel: + 44 (0) 1733 416477
www.thomascookpublishing.com

Produced by Cambridge Publishing Management Limited
Burr Elm Court, Main Street, Caldecote CB23 7NU

ISBN-13: 978-1-84157-978-8

First edition © 2008 Thomas Cook Publishing
Text © Thomas Cook Publishing
Maps © Thomas Cook Publishing/PCGraphics (UK) Limited

Project Editor: Karen Fitzpatrick
Production/DTP: Steven Collins

Printed and bound in Spain by GraphyCems

Front cover photography © Thomas Cook